LET'S BURN THE FLAGS OF ALL NATIONS

"Bold and inspiring, unyielding in their rigorous truth, Michael Brownstein's new poems work to transform habitual patterns of fear and greed into the sane and generous life we all deserve. *Let's Burn the Flags of All Nations* should be required reading for everyone."

Lynne Twist (*The Soul of Money*)

"These tough, uncompromising poems of witness, rage, and anarchic wit unmask the dysfunction of the human realm as it presses its Anthropocene agenda on the rest of the universe. They call for the end of patriarchy."

Anne Waldman (*Jaguar Harmonics*)

"Wonderful, powerful poems that excite the heart and reveal truths behind the so-called patriotism that feeds into the hands of the 1%."

John Perkins (*Confessions of an Economic Hit Man*)

"Michael Brownstein's new collection of poetry swings between melancholic epiphany and prophetic declamation as he explores the terminal direction and mystical hopes of our postmodern, trans-human times. This work sees through the spectral delusions of our age and points toward the potential for a planetary awakening into a state of unified consciousness and cooperative being. It is a worthy follow-up to his book-length proclamation, *World on Fire*."

Daniel Pinchbeck (*How Soon Is Now?*)

"Both bardic and vatic—that is, both poetic and prophetic—this book says truth with druidic intensity."

Peter Lamborn Wilson (*Ec(o)logues*)

"These heartfelt poems express the pain and beauty of being alive in this most challenging of times."

Starhawk (*Webs of Power*)

MICHAEL BROWNSTEIN

LET'S BURN THE FLAGS OF ALL NATIONS

DR. CICERO BOOKS

www.drcicerobooks.com

Dr. Cicero Books
New York Rio de Janeiro Paris
First Edition
Manufactured in the United States of America
Distributed by Small Press Distribution, Berkeley, CA

ISBN-13: 978-1-945766-16-9

for her

"The truth is, the old species is being broken apart so another possibility can emerge from it. And that's the key to everything."

Satprem, *Heart on Fire*

C O N T E N T S

CITATIONS

ACKNOWLEDGEMENTS

ABOUT THE AUTHOR

SO HERE WE ARE

The question is, "Now what?"

Will we slip the leash and be free of other-directed, biopathic, destructive forces or are we turning into denatured beings, GMO people, our genes saturated with plastic, our brains overflowing with microwaves?

Can we liberate ourselves from fictions fed to us since childhood about our bodies and minds, about who we are?

It could go either way.

But despite the demon realm still surrounding us a new consciousness is emerging, grassroots, optimistic, instantaneously in touch. A global phenomenon based on inclusion rather than separation.

As I heard on the street today, "Cooperative, communal, leaderless, open-source..."

POEMS

THIS POEM INCLUDES EVERYBODY

This poem includes everybody
Alive on the planet
At this very moment
What does that mean
How does it feel
And where will it take us
Our new worldwide body
Our new worldwide mind
Because have no doubt
It's either that or it's curtains
For the bubbly, cuddly
Ferocious human race

MY FRIENDS ALL TELL ME

My friends all tell me
They know who they are
But I find it hard to believe them
All I have to go on is me
And when I look in the mirror
I have no idea who I am
In fact, I've never known
Which gives me a leg up
Because although my friends
Can sense what's coming
Globally and personally
Their lives, their very identities
Turned upside down and inside out
Like a pretzel turning into a frog
They insist that life will go on
Pretty much the same as before
Why don't they see that if
We have no idea who we are
We can be whoever we want
Truckloads of stale biographies
Tilted into a psychic landfill
Our mothers never told us about
Because they had absolutely no idea
Who their little toddlers would soon become

LUCKY SHADOWS

for Laure

What if you and I
And whoever else
Had no last names
(Uh-oh, freedom calling)
New human emerging
Please take the time
Go inside, ask yourself
Maybe you'll see
We're just about
There already
Lucky shadows
Nothing more
Than our IP addresses
No last names
Anywhere on the planet
Can't be followed
By The Man anymore
In fact at this very moment
We're sailing out past the jetty
Into open ocean
Pure morning surrounds us
And if we're able to trust
You and me, us and them
There's nothing left to usurp
Sexual or otherwise
Open door, open field
No more power games
Partners forever
If that's what we want
Cause for the first time
In untold generations
We're simply here
No longer stick figures glued
To the board game of history
All the ancient cobwebs cleared away

The leaden suitcases filled
With dreary, outdated shit
We've been dragging around
Every last one of us
Auctioning ourselves off
To the highest bidder
Guarding our self-images
Our success and failure
A scorekeeper's paradise
What a relief, toss it overboard
Suitcases we swing
Out into boundless ocean
With the loudest roar
We've ever mustered
In this or any other lifetime
All our patterns and trips and excuses
Sinking into dark blue
Nothing left except
Our remarkably interesting faces
Vulnerable and open
Lucky shadows
On the new, improved internet
Still endless as the universe
But without any hardware at all
Sort of a two-way ESP
Mind to mind, soul to soul
What we lost
Thousands of years ago
(Uh-oh, freedom calling)
New human emerging
Can we get out of the way
Open to it, let it happen
Promise fulfilled
I'll be there too
First name Michael
Last time I looked

ON THE VERGE: ANONYMOUS AND COMMUNAL

"One crucial decision is likely to hold MixBit back: the video-sharing app is totally anonymous and communal. Users cannot post their videos under a name, and they cannot comment on each other's work." (The New York Times, August 8, 2013)

But will that indeed hold it back? Not if more and more people become anonymous and communal. Which is on the verge of happening. People already identify themselves by a mutating collection of usernames. Photoshopping their selfies. Concocting on-the-spot, temporary monikers. And once outdated memes like nine-to-five jobs, income tax, and national borders bite the dust, once pesky egos are meditated out of existence, what will remain besides happily sexual beings untethered from family history, racial history, national history? Far from their once-upon-a-time separate and paranoid identities. Anonymous and communal. Whirling through the dream of life like swarms of krill without end, swimming together in ecstasy in a nameless Antarctic sea.

EYE OF THE DOLPHIN

Twice in my life
I swam with bottlenose
dolphins in the Bahamas
years after having read
without thinking much
about it that dolphins
engage in intercourse
when the females are
not in their estrous cycles
and cannot produce young
in other words that they
mate purely for pleasure

Late on the final afternoon
of my second excursion
I was ten or twelve feet
below the surface peering
through my facemask
at a pod of bottlenose
when a huge and sleek
dark grey adult suddenly
peeled off from the rest
and raced toward me

Now inches from my face
an eye filled with supreme
ungovernable mischief
was staring at me and
I heard a voice saying
"Come play with us"
out of nowhere daring me
challenging me to join them
in the trackless ocean

And again that voice
preposterous, outlandish
"Come play with us"
big love without hesitation
big love without boundaries
with no thought for tomorrow
because there is no tomorrow
in the dreamtime ocean
no self-image to maintain
only gaiety beyond reckoning
freedom beyond imagining

Immediately I turned tail
fear starting to paralyze me
and swam as fast as I could
back to our fiberglass boat
bobbing in the waves
at least a mile out beyond
a tiny island with no name

Coughing and gasping
I let myself be pulled
up the rope ladder
by the leader of our group
a hard-bodied guy wearing
wraparound shades and
a digital wristwatch
and I saw what time it was
on this human afternoon
comprised of one set
of limitations after another

His wristwatch read 4:37
then it read 4:38 and 4:39
and I broke into tears on
the cramped, slippery deck
unable to free myself

from my skintight wetsuit
inconsolable to be fleeing
an impossible world
a world of play without end

FOR A POLYAMOROUS FRIEND

Here's a better way
let's say you're at the beach
throughout the morning

sunning, meditating
in perfect quiet, merged in space
with birds, ocean, sky

then, still lightly holding
that supra-individual identity
you're free to go

join the others
naked and beautiful
holding nothing back

free, calm, and open
to the agreed-upon place
of shade and refuge

tree branches and birdsong
where you lie down
and surrender, sleep

touch, make love
everything good with
one another, whoever's there

until late afternoon
when you return
if that's what you'd like

to the beach, continuing
the living dream
the dream worth living

PHYLLOTAXIS

thanks to John Martineau

Venus going around the Earth
Makes a flower shape
The sun sees

Everything perfectly
Organized and harmonic
All of this being
Aimed at us right now
As we begin to flower
Into consciousness

A quantum conscious universe
Trying everything at once
And getting it right

There isn't a circle
Going around the Earth
That's not harmonic
Electromagnetic signatures
Of all forms of life
Endocrine and brainwave

Patterns producing
Heightened dopamine
New ideas linked to the divine

LET'S BURN THE FLAGS OF ALL NATIONS

> *"I am a citizen of the world."* — *Diogenes*

Let's burn the flags of all nations
No more nation-states
No more patriotism
Try it, you'll like it

Welcome to the post-national future
Coming sooner than you think

Cause we've had enough
Of endless statements like this one
By India's Environment Minister
"National interest trumps all else"
Or this one by the President of Turkey
"No one should test the power of the state"

But why not test the power of the state
Why does an abstraction come before
The needs and desires of real people
What if there were no Israel, no China
No Indonesia, no Iran, no United States
Too radical for you

Maybe you'd rather remain a glutton
For punishment and continue swallowing
Non-negotiable declarations
Such as the following
"No government allows any organization
To interfere in its internal affairs"
This exact same phrase
Leaking out of the mouths
Of 6,733 nation-state lackeys
Since the beginning of patriarchal history

But nation-states are not the same as people
Mayans or Amazonians or Tibetans
Will get along perfectly well without
Artificial nation-states to define them
Because people don't wage war
Governments do
War presenting itself as necessary
For self-preservation when in fact
It's necessary for self-glorification

The modern nation-state is only
Four hundred years old and
What do nation-states do
They outlaw the teaching
Of indigenous languages, threaten
The survival of ethnic identities
They shut the door on our original past
Erasing cultural difference
Homogenizing everything for the
Benefit of the corporate state

The truth of the matter
Nationalism is a dead end
The nation-state is a criminal enterprise
Patriotism is a trick
And as long as we identify with nation-states
We know ourselves only by what we oppose
Not by who we are, and who are we
For a few years we're alive on this planet
Same heart, same mind, same eyes

Or do you keep turning a blind eye
To developments such as the following
A Botswana judge ruling that Bushmen
Who return to their ancestral lands
In the Central Kalahari Game Reserve
Are not allowed to drill wells for water

Meaning they have to walk up to
A hundred kilometers to fetch water
In one of the driest places on earth
While tourists who stay at the new
Tourist lodge on the reserve
Enjoy the use of swimming pool and bar
And Gem Diamonds' planned mine there
Will be free to take all the water it needs
On condition none is given to the Bushmen

Bushman spokesman Jumanda Gakelebone
"If we don't have water
How are we expected to live"
That is, how are they expected to live
Cut off from their immemorial life
As hunters and gatherers and herded into
Camps rife with alcoholism and violence
While aside from two tinhorn companies
Guess who profits from this crime, those
At the helm of Botswana's nation-state

No human illegal
No more national borders
Generated out of fear
Out of a total failure of trust
Arbitrary fictions
Laid down on a landscape
Borders which in reality don't exist
And if you believe they exist, tell me
What of all those who came before
Swearing fealty to other flags
At the cost of their lives
Down through history conquerors
Pillagers, colonizers, criminals
Who are we to claim any land is ours
Go back far enough
And we're all non-native species

We're all exotic reptiles loose
In a Florida of our own devising
Go back far enough
And everyone is illegal

Let's burn the flags of all nations
Release the stranglehold
Of the nation-state, cloud cover
For demagogues and racists
For America-firsters
Or Russia-firsters, etc.
What are they afraid of
That they'll melt
Into all us other humans
But like it or not
That's exactly what's happening
Reality of the internet
Everyone alive today
No fixed location
Floating in space
Just like the planet

No more nation-states
Benefiting those in power
Mimicking individual egos in combat
Battling for vanishing resources
For territory, *lebensraum*
Using the sentimental hook
Of tribal identification
To maintain order
The United States of America
A rank hallucination
Russia, Myanmar, Nigeria
You name it, hallucinations
Generated for profit and control
For suppression of the human spirit

But the human spirit
Knows no boundaries, no ID cards
No cradle-to-grave oversight
When we step outside the trance
And walk among the trees
Listen to the birds
Do we think they belong
To something called the US of A
Do they fall in line behind Old Glory

And around the globe
Hundreds of Old Glories
Each defended to the death
Tears streaming down the faces
Of patriots who drop their flag
Only to pick up a weapon
And murder those unlucky enough
To be carrying a different flag

Yes, it's against the law
To burn the flag in how many
Nation-states around the world
193 member states of the United Nations
From Afghanistan (when will we ever learn)
To Zimbabwe (the less said the better)
Outmoded nationalism
We're outgrowing it
No more electrified fences
Lit by floodlights of paranoia
No more making the nation-state
Safe for surveillance

And nationalism's obvious insanity
US ICBMs carrying nukes on
Hair-trigger alert, ready to launch
If early warning systems show
Incoming attack, these systems

Susceptible to false alarms, hacking
And human error, not to mention
All the other enemy-fixated
Nation-states out there
Armed with nuclear weapons
And following our lead

So no more patriots please
No more heads held high
Legitimizing a myth of separation
The myth that we humans
Who started as a single band
In the prehistoric night
Can now act only from our differences
Rationalizing mayhem and extermination
Forgetting who profits from separation
The corporate, political and military
Leaders of phantom entities
Founded in our name

Let's burn the flags of all nations
Either we join together
Or we're a bunch of dead pharaohs
Lined up in a row
Wrapped in shiny metallic tape
Reflecting our shriveled narratives
Back to us as we lie there not moving
In a cage instead of a playground

It's time to risk everything
Open the gates, tear down the fences
Roam wherever we like along
Rivers and mountains without end
Because we ourselves
Are those rivers and mountains

No human illegal

Syrians, Iraqis, Ethiopians
Mexicans, Guatemalans
Let them come
Let them swarm over Gringostan's borders
What are we afraid of
That they'll find out what we're really like
Afraid they'll compromise
The American way of life
But what is the American way of life
Everything for sale
Every last one of us hustling something
Caught in the opioid connective tissue
Of the American body politic
Methamphetamine trailers
Lighting up the high plains night
Strip malls from sea to shining sea
All for a second slice of virtual pizza
While the other nation-states out there
Are frantically copying us

But these *campesinos*
Why are they pouring across our borders
If their village-based mode of survival
Were still functioning
After corporate capital's
Scorched earth policy, after
The bait and switch called Free Trade
After the drug violence fueled
By our own cocaine habit
After the bombs falling out of the sky
Do you really think they'd leave
Their families and ancestral lands
For a life of drudgery
In the icy heart of the North

Can you imagine what those
Who've risked their lives to cross

The border are thinking as they
Clean our toilets and mow the lawns
Outside our cheesy McMansions
While we sprawl in the family room
Sucking up doses of radiation
From our plasma screens, our big-ass
TVs with each year higher and higher
Resolution until one fine day
We can't tell the difference between
Who we are and what we see

But what if, on the contrary
The *campesinos* secretly envy us
What if they want their deracinated children
To grow into big-time consumers
Just like us, what if
They can't wait till their kids
Get lost in celebrity culture
Turning into dark-skinned versions
Of our tight white selves
Dios mio...

Maybe they will even swallow
The myth of American exceptionalism
Our benevolent hegemony, our moral
Superiority and unique good intentions
Our special standing in the eyes of God
All of it no more than a flat-out fantasy
Variations of which have appeared
Over and over in nation-states from
Ancient Sumer to the storm-tossed present
Leaving us swept away by an ever-growing
Number of fulminating bipolar patriots

And democracy, our claim to fame
Time for a reality check
In this post-truth era voting means

Getting lost in make-believe
Whenever we're more than 10,000 people
Approximate size of the *polis*
In ancient Greece where citizens
Met one another face to face
Knew their strengths and foibles
Knew the skeletons in their closets
Their families and ancestors

Whereas who represents us now
Holograms assembled by layers
Of spin doctors and handlers
For a Potemkin media village
Built only to impress and if
You doubt it (and have enough pull)
Approach the leader of any nation-state
It doesn't matter
What his or her politics are
The only question is
How deep into trance is this person
Wave your hand in front of the face
Watch the eyes light up
When you say you'll vote for it
Watch the eyes go cold
When you say you won't

Not to mention how the fix is in
By means of voter suppression
The 2016 US presidential election
Skewed by tricks like Crosscheck
Secret purge list accusing
7.2 million blacks and Latinos
With similar names of being
Registered to vote in two states
Whereupon their names were
Removed from the voter rolls

And not to mention the new
Bot propaganda campaigns
By weaponized AI machines
Resulting in automated behavior
Through personality profiling
Resulting in physical
And psychological misdirection
The latest bright and shiny version
Of a consensus reality that's been
Drummed into our heads for centuries

But life can be radically different
In fact at this very moment
Though mortally threatened on all sides
The Rojava Revolution is alive
Democratic confederalism in northern Syria
Three cantons translating resistance
Against state oppression into a new
Political model of stateless democracy
Inspired by the Kurdish Women's Movement
Social ecology rejecting the nation-state
Dispensing with the oppressive structure
Of patriarchal capitalism and instead
Basing itself on co-existence

Afrin, Cizire, and Kobane
A confederation of autonomous regions
Kurds, Arabs, Assyrians, Chaldeans
Arameans, Turkmen, Armenians, Chechens
And although for now Afrin has fallen
To the Turkish nation-state
Cizire is surviving and Kobane
Almost perished but Kobane
Is surviving and nothing will erase
The dream of democratic confederalism

Meanwhile back stateside

Left and right, red and blue
Enforce the age-old delusion
That we can get somewhere
Only at the expense of others
But haven't you noticed
The game is never won
Over the centuries always a sense
Of impending emergency
Of corruption and betrayal
The open field of existence
Tricked into gigantic hoardings
Of mine and yours

The question is
Do we have what it takes
To clear the deck
And work out a new life

That's the only reason astronauts
Were allowed up in space
To see global intelligence unfolding
A vast display of ecologies
Humans and plants
Animals and spirits
Sky and ocean

No more nation-states
No more patriotism
Try it, you'll like it

THAT OLD GREY SUN

That old grey sun
tangled up in his pantyhose
looking for a pair of scissors
looking to break free
from the same stony planets
circling him over and over again
especially the one called Earth
what a huge disappointment
liars and thieves and murderers
infiltrating that radiant world
for a hundred centuries
like a creepy imitation
of the joyful shining gods
the sun was hoping for when
all golden in anticipation
he first saw men and women
emerge out of virgin jungle
before they started running
as fast as humanly possible
and then even faster than that
around an endless racetrack
somewhere inside their minds

GIGANTIC HALLUCINATION

This is all a gigantic hallucination
Including your favorite restaurant
Including the trash on the street
Being collected by the new tireless robots
Including the exact same bills coming
Due month after month like black magic
Including row after row of petty tyrants
Flexing their biceps in the blazing heat
Just look around you, it's delusional
On the grandest scale imaginable
To take one up-to-the-minute example
The genius billionaires of Silicon Valley
Having long ago rejected the invisible
Having ignored the realm of spirit
Having ridiculed the Goddess
Are so afraid of looking death in the eye
They're spending their brief lives
Trying to figure out a way to live forever
They insist on squandering their billions
Building rocket ships to another world
Now that they've helped to ruin this one
With a paralyzing combination of
Ravenous ego and cocky technology
They want to maroon themselves
On some cold uninhabitable planet
Where they'll live for thousands of years
And drive one another nuts
Over and over and over again

JUST BEFORE DUSK

Cities across this strangest of planets
Filled with billions of people
Tearing around in battered taxis
Their eyes glued to the meter

Or maybe they're at home
Eyes forever glued to something
Their kids, their bills, the clock
The television, the computer constantly
Pulling them outside of themselves

And the skulls beneath their grinning faces
Become visible late in the day
Just before dusk
Sugar-coated skulls glowing briefly
During strolls through fading light
Down littered, noisy avenues

Long before they finally quit the scene
They've given up the ghost
To something always inches away
Eyes glued to the meter
Even in dreams
Even during sex
And me, am I any different
And you

SHORT POEM IN THE FORM OF A QUESTION

They shared
everything
in prehistory

Their bodies
their lives
their destiny

Why not us
right here
right now

AFTER PATRIARCHY COLLAPSES AND CAPITALISM CRUMBLES

"They did not know it was impossible, so they did it" — *Mark Twain*

After patriarchy collapses
And capitalism crumbles
We won't be wage slaves anymore
Instead we'll do whatever brings
The famous archaic smile of prehistory
To our lips and that's what we'll
Call work because after patriarchy
Collapses and capitalism crumbles
Greed will melt away like evil ice cream
Leaving no trace, not even in museums
And with confident, unarmored hearts
We'll gladly share what we have
With whoever shows up at our door
As long as the light of what used to be
Called God shines in their eyes

After patriarchy collapses
And capitalism crumbles
An easygoing form of baseball
Will be the prevailing sport and we
Won't care much who wins or loses
Because all of us, players and spectators
Will succumb to the mystical dimensions
Of the game, and after patriarchy collapses
And capitalism crumbles, significant others
Of every possible sexual inclination
Will trust the way physical intimacy
Brings out the best in us
Because who's kidding whom
We're alive for a limited time only
And we own no one
And no one owns us

After patriarchy collapses
And capitalism crumbles
We'll get lost in each other's
Trickster bodies and minds
Free to touch and let go
Touch and let go, sliding in
And out of kaleidoscopic embrace
As we make our way through
All of eternity like the stars
Like the clouds and the wind
Finding that our finicky personas
Matter less than we suppose

After patriarchy collapses
And capitalism crumbles
We'll lead a life we can barely
Imagine now, a strategy developed
Tens of thousands of years ago
By two-leggeds who roamed
Through jungles and forests, their
Longhouse kids raised communally
Leaving room for a wide-open journey
Without our usual rage for control
While making sure to care for
And pleasure everyone

After patriarchy collapses
And capitalism crumbles
Nation-states will disappear
Humans streaming back and forth
Across abandoned customs checkpoints
Sharing skin colors and songs
Copyrighted by no one while we
Mingle on a never-ending playground
Stretching across the face of the Earth
A panorama without zoos or prisons
Without addiction to the profit motive

Without spending our productive years
Amassing and then guarding wealth

After patriarchy collapses
And capitalism crumbles
We'll be closing in on
Clear-eyed, gracious, humble lives
At last finding a way to be sane
Together on this psychoactive planet
("Heal me Mama, Mama heal me")
While from far and wide
Throughout the infinite universe
Alien beings on millions of worlds
Beyond the constraints of space and time
Will look down at us in wonder
At what we've been able to pull off
Against all odds
And applaud

MIRROR, MIRROR ON THE WALL

There's a guy who I once knew
Always kept himself in shape
Working out before the mirror
Pushed himself, running late

He had a chance to be a winner
Make his mom break down and cry
He had his mind set on the future
Perfect body in his eye

Then one day he woke up crazy
Crashing like a wrecking ball
He looked inside and came up empty
Mirror, mirror on the wall

He saw the game that he was playing
But what was even more
He saw that no one else was watching
No one else was keeping score

WE AMERICANS ARE FREE

We Americans are free
We're free to pull out of our driveways
And return
We're free to watch the big storm develop on TV
And then tell our friends that we survived it
We're free to demonstrate in the streets
For a sane and open-hearted system
With equal rights for all forms of life
As long as we don't make a sound
And the rest of America ignores us

And we Americans are free
To make sure that all of our children
The ones who will inherit our furniture
Go to bed with spikes in their arms
Filled with a weird kind of jelly
Which by the time they're of voting age
Makes them fall in love with the bottom line
And salute a flag whose red is blood
Whose white are bones
And whose blue is sheer dissociation

THINGS YOU CAN'T GOOGLE

You can't Google what your mother
whispered in your father's ear
at the moment of your conception
and you can't Google how your father
struggled for years to break free from
the numbing routine that buried him

You can't Google why your mother
smothered you as a child with her love
changing the course of the universe forever
in a way no astronomer is able to explain
and you can't Google where the innocence
of children went or why five-year-olds
are fiercely competitive and covered
with brand names from head to foot

You can't Google why you blew it
with the guy or gal who meant more
to you than anyone else you ever met
and who you've lost track of for decades
in spite of looking for him or her always

You're unable to Google how uneasy you are
about growing old alone no matter how many
people surround you, because you can't Google
why only at the moment of your passing will
your loved ones look up from their screens

You can't Google how much you hate the sound
of mice trapped in the walls of your little castle
swaying in the solar wind and you can't Google
how far it is in interstellar space before you reach
the refuge of a jolly and hospitable planet

You can't Google the identity of the entities
crowding around the windows of your castle
making faces at you and laughing while you
slowly run out of food and water and air
or why the last black rhinoceros is made
to disappear so that some insecure male
on cruise control can fool himself about
the priapic qualities of powdered rhino horn

You can't Google why William Blake seeing
heaven in a grain of sand has been replaced
by you seeing hell in a grain of plastic and
you can't Google why poetry might be the only
pure product left, poets like sacred prostitutes
giving it all away, while the rest of the world
drives a harder and harder and harder bargain

But it's also true there's no way to Google
the adamantine mystery of life, why the plant
realm is so helpful to us or why monkeys
in the jungle defecate with ease while
humans in cities remain hopelessly constipated
and for sure you can't Google if the fact that
we see so many colors is proof of God's existence

HUSHED-UP COROLLARY

Hushed-up corollary
Unintended side-effect
Of the broadband revolution
Our mobile-device era
Undeniable gift of the internet
Free communication
Instantaneous information
Evading control structures
Suddenly crowds materialize
Out of nowhere
Against the corrupt status-quo
Hundreds of thousands in the streets
Ukraine, the Middle East, India

But the hushed-up corollary
Already happening in offices
And bedrooms around the planet
Hormonal disruption
Sexes scrambled, estrogen
Dominance through the roof
Isolated priapic episodes
Bolt upright in your cubicle
Not to be denied
Office or no office
Racing after anything
With a hole in it
But mostly the exact opposite
An epidemic
Males deflating
Impotence, sterility, big breasts
In Great Britain for example
Over the last decade
20% less sexual activity
Flaccid penises

Their owners flipping out
Turning to testosterone creams
Patches, pills, injections
Turning to Viagra, to red meat
Anything to stem the tide
Not stopping to think
At home and at work
Always in the company
Of our new little friends
Tablets and smartphones and laptops
Never inquiring about EMFs
Like the so-called smart meters
Installed by power companies
On the other side of the wall
Against which you're trying to sleep
While in Japan young adults
Losing interest in sexual intimacy
Rather play with their devices
Go shopping with their pals

All of this just the beginning
The entrée, the threshold
Where did our love go
Our health, our well-being
Can't get no satisfaction
And not only men
More and more women
Wondering how and why
Breast cancer rates spiking
Environmental toxins of course
Ubiquitous plastics, fake food
But what else
Not realizing
Hormones skewed, disrupted
Pledging allegiance
To the mobile-device era
Routers, deck phones, microwaves

Unintended side-effect
Hushed-up corollary
Hugging technology so close
Like a lover, like a soulmate
Magnetized by our devices
Can't seem to back away
Collective trance
Are you experienced
Drug without a drug
Trojan Horse, tasty seclusion
Do you Twitter, do you Facebook
Either you're in or you're out
High school all over again
From Toronto to Tierra del Fuego
From Cairo to Burundi
From Moscow to Mongolia
From Beijing to Bali
Undeniable gift, yes
Improving so many lives
And yet – and yet

One thing's for sure, though
A new generation
Of human is arriving
A kind of cyborg
Part flesh, part electronic device
And in this painful period of transition
Until the kinks get ironed out
Your partner lies beside you in bed
His or her heart aching
His or her eyes
Turned away in frustration
Looking out the nighttime window
At the glittering, untouchable stars

WHY I LEFT THE CITY

More and more
People on the street
Being erased
Right before my eyes
There he is
There she is
One moment scrunching
Into a smartphone
The next moment gone
Without a trace
Not even a shoe
Or a sock
Left behind

IMPOSSIBLE THINGS ARE HAPPENING

Impossible things are happening
human marsupials sort of
wandering around my neighborhood
legally defined as normal adults
with their addicted adolescent sidekicks
all of them gestating not babies
but clever new electronic devices
in their cool and drooping pouches

They keep walking and walking
but they can't find whatever it is
they claim they're looking for
they're restless automatons sort of
no longer comfortable in their skins
something got into the water
something got into the food
something got into the air

Guess I'll have to live with it
what other choice do I have
as long as my feet are on the ground
as long as my head is in the clouds
as long as my heart is in my throat
but will someone please tell me
what's really going on here
are we still human beings sort of

Or what

ZOMBIE APOCALYPSE

The zombie
apocalypse
is drawing
near
it first
manifests
at what
seems
the most
unlikely
of places
a Friday night
high school
football game
deep in
the heart
of Texas
and you
can't help
noticing
that it
indeed
is there
and nowhere
else
because
no matter
how many
touchdowns
are scored
quarter
after quarter
after quarter
after quarter
the scoreboard
keeps reading

zero
to zero
and as
the hours
and days
the weeks
and months
and years
roll by
in what we
laughingly
still
refer to
as time
no one
at that game
gets up from
their seats
and leaves
the stadium
no one
yells
or cheers
or boos
they simply
sit there
transfixed
not unlike
what you
and I
will do
when this
empty cloud
slowly turns
and moves
our way

ROBOCENTURY YES NO

"I'm not a robot"
we keep insisting
and yes that's true
as far as it goes
we're made of flesh
we're made of blood
we laugh and cry
with great certainty
except maybe when
we have to answer
the following question
who or what is listening

THE NEAR FUTURE

In 1800 in all the world
there were one billion people
in 1950, two billion
now there's seven and a half billion
ten billion people by the year 2025
exploding, spurting, surging
tidal wave, earthquake, blink of an eye
how many is too many?
what will the word "human" mean
in 2025, not that far away, really
when everybody will be in possession
of one little room the size of their heads
dreaming revelatory dreams of
the world filled to bursting with humans
in the year 1800, the year 1950
the years 2025, 2250, 3137, 483632
wherever "now" went
whoever's "here" now
scratching our heads, trying
to make sense of our success

Because for humans it turns out
winning also means losing
losing folkways, losing space
losing the unknown
whoever's "alive" now
whatever "dead" means
as you turn to me and insist
"I've got a grip on things now"
but actually the grip's on you
population density altering identity
warping thought patterns
pasteurizing consciousness, making us
forget that every moment in history
is flush with prehistory
is full of acid flashbacks

of us dropping down out of the trees
sniffing the air, feet planted on the ground
loving the sights, the sounds of earthly life
someone builds a fire and we all gather round
looking each other in the eye
embracing every last person in the circle
big smiles on our faces
for a hundred thousand years

But today the tables have turned
critical mass, demographic flash point
irradiated, plastic-saturated, genetically
modified people spilling over the rim
uncountable as microbes
especially when you factor in
our multiple personalities, our vast
entourage of memories and demons
and our self-images ain't working too good
neither, even though we're afraid
to drop the dead hand of ownership—
competitive, property-worshipping
suspicious, conspiratorial, anti-feminine
feeling up the planet for the hell of it

Private property solidifying mistrust
monogamy, the work ethic, clock time
billionaire fortunes, destitution
they're suffocating us until
our only option is surrender
no more me owning you, you owning me
until we float away from our armored selves
like deep sea divers releasing their harpoons
mental nomads erasing the space
between here and there, between now and then
between you and me
otherwise we keep hardening and shrinking
all ten billion of us, all 30 billion, 50 billion

Because the age of smallness is fast approaching

a perfect little cube we call home
with a few houseplants that stand for the jungle
dusty terrariums we'll think of as the wilderness
while we christen a puddle under the kitchen sink
the Great Salt Lake—
look, see the bonsai trees on the mall
see the tiny automobiles driving around
down there below the matchstick bridge
wherever they go, they always arrive
they never get lost, there's no way to get lost
everyone's options screwed on tight
people jammed against the walls
dangling from the rafters
lining the hallways of each other's dreams

But there's still a voice calling to us
from deep inside our bones
saying smallness is not our fate
super high density signaling
the next big flash point
breakthrough into resonance
new ways of seeing and feeling
and although you may not know it
the trees on the hillsides watching
our game are beside themselves
with joy, they've waited so long
for this moment when marauding
humans have the chance to come home
and start thinking the way plants
and animals have always thought
every life form on Earth dissolving
the distance between here and there
between now and then
between you and me

NOW WHAT

Now that I realize my life is a dream
Now what
Now that I know I'll be gone soon
My time on this planet drawing to a close
What really matters to me
Cause I don't give a fuck
About the Tribeca Film Festival
While so many plants and animals
Are disappearing and the world's
Third largest dam is being built in Brazil
Obliterating tribal cultures like a tsunami
To make the world safe for soybeans
I don't give a hoot about the new iPhone
Or the hundreds of millions of people
Falling in love with themselves on Instagram
While the Great Pacific Garbage Patch
Turns a collection of plastic junk
Twice the size of Texas into tiny pellets
Ingested by the smaller fish out there
Which then are eaten by the larger fish
Caught in the nets of floating factories
Looking to satisfy our seemingly
Limitless hunger for sushi
I turn away from this dumb-show
And ask myself now what
Now that I've figured out
This life is a dream, the world
As we know it a flash in the pan
Fool's gold
Now that I understand
Now what

COMING UP FOR AIR

Sometimes I get so upset
What are we doing to the world
What are we doing to ourselves
Stupid, vain, cruel, greedy, lost
So upset I forget who I am
Until I tell myself
Breathe, just breathe
Come back into your body
Let go of mental efforting
Come up for air

Return to pure awareness
Empty and luminous
Original mind as vast as the sky
Before judgments and perceptions
Who's right and who's wrong
And I remember
To exchange chi with the universe

I lie down on the floor
Stretch out my legs
With my feet naturally apart
Draw my eyesight into my eyes
Lower my eyelids and inhale
Absorbing chi from all directions
To every part of my body
Then exhale
From every part of my body
To the universe

I do this thirty-six times
Lying on a piece of cloud
Floating in the blue sky
The sun casting its warm rays on me

I feel the gentle touch of the breeze
I am with nature
I am with the universe
I am nature
I am the universe

ANCIENT ANIMAL PRESENCE

Way I've been
standing lately
don't want to lose it
just standing
knees bent
shoulders rounded
but no tension, feeling
heat in lower dan tien
chi in the center
of my feet, at ease
in this loose solidity
sheer physical certainty
this alert and focused
ancient animal presence
moving only if necessary
but in another sense
always moving
swaying, rolling, breathing
nothing on my mind
nothing in my head

TREES ARE MY FAVORITE KIND OF PEOPLE

Trees are my favorite kind of people
In the late fall I discover
A massive red oak in the forest
Gold leaves ankle-deep on the ground

At least two hundred years old
Anchored in the dream
Mature and healthy paragon
Formidable presence

More present than me that's for sure
More present than anyone I know
Locked in without effort
Forever slow and sweet

I approach her
As calmly as I can
When I finally quiet down
A spirit emerges

Don't know what else to call it
From the thickest part of the trunk
From heart level
And if my heart opens

If I surrender
Healing beyond words
And deeper than that
Naked awareness

Unconditional love I feel then
For everyone I've ever known
Whether or not I care about them
Whether or not they care about me

THE SOUND OF THE FOREST

The sound
Of the forest
Cannot be
Put into words
Except after the
Loggers have come
Then you can put it
Into one word
"Gone"

BIG DILEMMA

This wild hillside
beside a summertime lake
popular with families
makes me come alive
out beyond words
my eyes go soft
my mouth goes slack
my body starts to shake
I smell and feel and hear
the life force density
pouring off these nameless plants
the same signals they've been sending
for hundreds of millions of years
but to be truly at ease here
with no one else around
where I take my clothes off
naked for hours on end if I like
I would have to own this lake
and own the mountains around it
and the mountains around those mountains
I'd have to have hundreds of millions
of dollars, and to do that
what kind of head would I be in
I'd be corrupt and paranoid
I'd start ordering the servants around
the imaginary servants
I'd turn into an ancient Greek tyrant
and the gods above would grow angry
they'd be sure to cut me down to size
and let me loose once again
naked and peevish and poverty-stricken
on the shore of this summertime lake
crowded with chatterbox adults
lost in reactivity and distraction

with their screaming dogs
their barking children
and their proxy music machines
the latest in up-to-date humans
more primitive in their own way
if primitive means undeveloped
than the waves of insects
locked in perpetual resonance
filling this wild hillside with song

SPIRITS

The invisible is real

Spirits miss us
They want us back
But only if we
Miss them too, only
If we meet them with
Humility and gratitude

But they do miss us
They want us singing
They want us back inside
Where humans and plants
Spirits and animals
Speak the same language

"I once had a dream that wasn't a dream"

And why not admit it
We have no clue
What life will be like
A hundred years from now
When the little girl asks
"Daddy, what was the Fourth of July?"

"Must've been a dream within a dream"

While we spend our time
Either on the other line
Or away from our desk
We miss surrendering to
Those ancient power voices
Inside ourselves once again

"Yes, we want you back with us"

THE JEWISH POEM

Can we find our way back
I mean all the way back
before a jealous G-d
before Abraham and Sarah
wandered off from Sumer
before ancient Sumer itself
gave birth to patriarchy
scourge of the planet
ushering in the end times
before David and Solomon
before priests and kings
before Jewish exceptionalism
but not before
the original Shekinah
divine feminine presence
body of light, body of bliss
incarnation of the Goddess
when we Jews were
a tribe like any other

Tribes speaking in tongues
wearing rainbow IDs
of skin and meat and bone
hunters and gatherers
shakers and trance dancers
Jews no different
moving with the seasons
year after year, circling
around, starting over
owning next to nothing
burning our self-images
in great bonfires determined
by configuration of the stars
burning fixations and regrets

burning bruised egos
burning lingering grudges
burning effigies of hate
sending it all up in flames
egalitarian and free
at home in telepathy
and celebration, at ease
in our animal bodies

Because Judaism
not even a religion
till forced to survive
slavery in Egypt by
sheer mountain magic
till forced to survive
Roman defeat by
mimicking the Romans
till forced to survive
the scorched-earth policy
of medieval Christians
by adopting Catholic
sterile male absolutism
by hiding our wizardry
in secret Kaballah texts
by abandoning our
pantheistic pagan roots
for a trickle-down religion
where we finally became
respectable cut-out figures
in the fully urbanized
pop-up book of anti-life

Instead original tribal
Judaism a free-wheeling
shamanic assemblage
of wonder-working rabbis
healing the sick and lame

invoking the spirit world
overflowing with visions
can we find our way back
to long before biblical
brick and mortar holy land
can we return
to life before patriarchy
before a distant sky G-d
before thou shalt not, before
all the rules and regulations
the obsession with purity
before the terrible swift sword
before the commandment
to massacre in cold blood
every last tribe around us
with whom we shared
what we called Canaan

Before the Promised Land
before fear and trembling
before we were tossed
from the Garden in shame
before the Garden itself
before storerooms bursting
with grain, slave food for
monuments built by forced
labor, before egomaniacal
kings and queens, before
herds of tame animals and
the killer military needed
to defend them, before
one culture after another
shoved the Goddess aside
before we got hoodwinked
into forsaking wilderness
fleeing from Shekinah
to whom we had always

willingly surrendered
outside of clock time
outside of history

From the Mediterranean Sea
to the Bay of Bengal
and beyond, the Goddess
as old as the hills
she belonged to nobody
she belonged to everybody
radiating her power
her sexual arousal
taking preference over
all else, men gladly
performing yoga-tattva
down on their knees
worshipping her sex
which in full-on trance
her legs spread wide
she displayed for all to see
holding back nothing
and the non-stop hunger
of men made perfect sense
then, and everyone was
satisfied, everyone complete

This is what we lost
when Big Boy took over
men shielding themselves
from women who became
no more than servants
no more than baby factories
as we slammed the lid shut
over ecstasy until Christians
and Moslems outdid us
carpet-bombing sexuality
replacing her presence

with nuclear-tipped rockets
sacrificing everything
we held dear, love and
sanity and well-being
at the altar of patriarchy

So say it again, we Jews
a tribe like any other
born from undulations
of the feminine landscape
for untold thousands of years
supplicants in sacred groves
our ceremonies shamanic
glorying in our physicality
luscious, at ease, conversing
with spirits, eating truth-
telling psychoactive plants
fucking in the bushes
big smiles on our faces
any day of the week
any week of the year

No guilt, no fear
of G-d's searchlight
swinging down from above
keeping an eye on us
a monstrous fiction
concocted by an upstart
priestly caste solely for
control and corruption
signaling the end
of the old ways
signaling the beginning
of fanatical suspicion
of the bad news
known as Almighty G-d

And in short order
there we were
scurrying along below Him
no longer making way
for the Goddess in our
midst, no longer greeting
our brothers and sisters
the plants and animals
no longer our divine selves
but bowing and scraping
before a G-d perpetually
jealous of His own creation
while we surrendered our
mojo in an attempt to
placate and please Him
our paternalistic G-d
our angry G-d
approving this and smiting that
full of ascetic fury, a fury
identical to the barren unforgiving
desert from whence He came

When Yahweh, single true god
of the entire world, gave orders
to wipe out every last heathen
how different were we
from the desert religions
materializing after us
how different from 4th century
to 21st century Christianity
how different from 7th century
to 21st century Islam
zealots citing chapter and verse
to justify mayhem
to justify extermination
all of us born from the sand
from punishing heat and

a vacant sky delivering nothing
monotheisms outlawing pleasure
drowning Shekinah in her bath
disowning the here and now
carving up eternity into
house lots and freeways
promising only the possibility
of a reward in faraway heaven
once we're dead and gone

CHRIST THE QUEEN

Jesus the Jew
who fearlessly embodies
Christ consciousness
throughout the universe
from the beginning of time
till Doomsday plus one
was actually a woman
in fact the only woman
who has ever existed

She was crucified
after having her breasts
removed by surgeons
at the beck and call
of militant male powers
in order to pave the way
for a so-called Christian
church secretly functioning
as the lid on the sepulcher
of the Goddess triumphant

There are very few hard
and fast facts in the satanic
mill or jelly-like hall
of mirrors we persist in
calling history but surely
one of the most undeniable
is that nowhere do we find
mention or depiction of
the penis of Christ and this
for the best of reasons
namely, there is none

Of course it's true that
long after the faithful

had been taught to view
male oppression
as natural and right
nothing came easier
than to portray the
infant Jesus complete
with visible boy member
in one Madonna and
Child after another

But please look closely with
unbiased gaze at any statue
or painting of the Christ
nailed high up on the cross
and you will see tiny
almost invisible scars
on her chest and you will
realize the only possible
direction left for us poor
pugnacious earthlings in
this dickbrain day and age
is unconditional surrender
to the one who came before

GODDESS MEMORIES

Once upon a time
For various divine
Heterosexual practices
There used to be
Various kinds of males
And the question was
Which male would
Be most beneficial
For which practice
But now in this
Degenerate age
When divine sexuality
No longer exists there's
Only one kind of male
And his ignorance
Apparently knows no bounds

HERE COMES KALI MA

Can everybody hear me
I don't mean just in this room
I mean in the whole boxed-in world
Because we're running out of time
It's now or never
And I have one last thing to say
Please don't take it personally
Please don't be offended
But yes there is a Kali Ma
And she's fixing to kick ass
She has no hesitation or regrets
She's losing patience
Faster and faster
Do you feel her losing patience
She's ready to throw in the towel
The towel with all of our names on it
She wants us to open up and surrender
Do you see her coming toward you
Fierce and loose and fearless
Do you see her fabulous smile
Her fangs dripping with blood
Her eyes triumphant and remote
Do you hear her saying it's time
Time for every last one of us
To start over again from scratch
Now she reaches out to you
Are you brave enough to deal with it
She's tickling your ribs, she's sticking
Her tongue right down your throat
She needs you to drop everything
Let your guard dogs run free
Drop all your labels and excuses
Embrace her like there's no tomorrow
Because there is no tomorrow
There's only now or never

SACRED TRASH

Mayan trickster friend
Antonio O by name
Body worker, shaman
Huckster, untrustworthy
Lover all rolled into one
He and I were riding
Rattletrap bus that day
Me in the window seat
Him on the aisle through
The wilds of Oaxaca

Just past a blaring town
I looked out the window
Hillside dropping straight
To a skinny creek below
Choked with mounds of
Trash, refuse, broken TVs
Smoking tires, dead cats
And though I'd seen
Similar scenarios more
Than once in Mexico

This time it hit me
Suddenly I was depressed
Yet another garbage dump
Violating pristine nature
And I turned to Antonio
My cheeks wet with tears
Until his eyes glittering
He flashed the biggest smile
In all of creation and sang out
"Sacred trash, Miguelito!"

ON OUR OWN

Seeing how
to proceed
in the present
by relating
to the past
becomes more
and more difficult
as the scope
of our identity
keeps widening
and shrinking
until it stretches
around the globe
thin as the coating
of functional material
on a semiconductor
device and we
no longer will admit
that without
a living tradition
instead of sterile
rationalism
(and the family thing
doesn't quite do it)
without a deep
and ancient past
where we contact
spirits of earth and sky
to whom we
can surrender
our near-sighted egos
we are submerged
in a crowd
and getting older

day by day
maddening
excruciating
because everyone
seems to be
playing a game
of not noticing
time has them
has us all
by the throat

THROUGH THE LOOKING GLASS

During these liminal times
when everything is overlapping
and the bottom drops out
reality is still always richer
than we're making use of
so in spite of our misgivings
we become threshold people
entering the looking glass
where normally accepted
convictions and conventions
and social class barriers
fall away, allowing a structure
of *communitas* to appear
based on common humanity
equality instead of hierarchy
while the mirror we were using
to confirm ourselves dissolves
causing disorientation vertigo
but also a fresh start
and this is good news
the bright new world
we all deserve and crave

But navigating choppy
full-on global rites of passage
if we don't have the guidance
of a master of ceremonies
a tribal elder whose ancient
rituals can safely lead us
through the looking glass
allows schizoid tricksters to appear
self-proclaimed ceremony masters
deranged, pitiless, without fear
unable to trust or give or share

(remind you of anyone?)
who assume leadership positions
exploiting our dislocation and
hypnotizing the faint of heart
while the brave ones among us
manage to stand at the crossroads
of identity and time, watching
the dead centuries fall away
dissolving old ghost memories
which gives us great hope
for the bright new world
we all deserve and crave

In our present-day liminality
without a master of ceremonies
received opinions and traditions
educated guesses and percentages
all turn into gobbledegook
and the future is wilderness
the fabled far side of
an unnameable moon where
schizoid tricksters mimic charismatics
using decisive word and image
and supremely confident behavior
to block our way through
freezing us on the surface
of the looking glass itself
while they harvest our uncertainty
like so much ripened grain
for what seems forever and a day
counterfeiting *communitas*
and obscuring the bright new world
we all deserve and crave

But though glacially ignored
spirit guides still do exist
bears and hawks and shorebirds

panthers, bats and dolphins
border animals inhabiting sacred
places betwixt and between
springs, caves, shores and rivers
high mountains touching the sky
in that time beyond time
before and after the dead centuries
such spirits serving as beacons
for the master of ceremonies
who—it's up to us
we either re-discover right quick
among the few original people
hidden away on this planet
or invent anew to lead us
far from schizoid tricksters
and through the looking glass
to *communitas*, where life
is spacious and loving and
above all makes sense
the bright new world
we all deserve and crave

IF YOU SEE SOMETHING, SAY SOMETHING

(NYC, 2006)

We need your help as an extra set of eyes and ears
Unattended bags? Suspicious behavior? Take notice
Of people in bulky or inappropriate clothing
Report anyone tampering with video cameras
Or entering unauthorized areas
If you see something, say something

I see something
I see a criminally insane person
Roaming the halls of the White House
He believes he's the president of the United States
And I see a rotund bastard with a heart problem
Hovering in the background, pulling the strings
His crooked smile lights the way to perdition

In the early morning chill I see New York streets
Filled with people on their way to work
We say we're safe because John Ashcroft retired
No more red alerts, no more terrorists disguised
As tourists worming their way into town, no more
Dirty bombs left in suitcases in Grand Central
Little do we know, little dare we surmise

As the rotund bastard with the heart problem
Said the other day, "It's not an accident
That we haven't been hit in five years"
What's that supposed to mean, that sooner
Or later he'll feel threatened enough
To provoke the crazies into action
And when he does will he be in his secret
Climate-controlled tunnel half-way
Between D. C. and Wyoming
Far from the narrow, dark canyons of Manhattan

If you see something, say something
I see something
I see the forgotten anthrax killers
Whose bio-weapons source
Was not al-Qaeda but our own American arsenals
I see no global war declared on Fort Detrick or
The Dugway Proving Grounds, no troops deployed
No actions taken, our attention always focused
Somewhere out there (Iraq, Iran, North Korea)
Never in here

If you see something, say something
I see a billion dollars a week spent on this war
Rather than the two billion a year needed
To lock down leaking Russian nuclear facilities
I see the U.S. military buying anthrax
In violation of treaties limiting the spread
Of bio-weapons, I see nanotech embraced
For mirage medical cures while its use for
Surveillance and control is ignored, I see
All of us inoculated into a state
Of permanent low-level paranoia

If you see something, say something
I see something
I see our Supreme Leader in the Oval Office
Fondling "the football," the top-secret suitcase
With instructions to blow up the planet
Sixteen years after the Berlin Wall fell
I see thousands of hydrogen bombs
Still on hair-trigger alert in Russia and the USA
I see forty of those bombs aimed at New York City

If you see something, say something
I see our protective coating of ironic distance
Shielding us from the truth

Over the phone I hear "Have a nice day"
And "Please speak to the system"
And in the stores, behind the Christmas carols
I hear the whine of black helicopters
Making the world safe for demonocracy
"Freedom!" I bark, and a miniature poodle
On a leash barks back at me

I see something
I see the U.S. holding the world for ransom
Again and again the same words keep surfacing
"In the national interest, in the national interest"
Reptilian brains having a toxic over-reaction
To testosterone, plunging all of us
Into the icy waters of selfish calculation

If you see something, say something
I see this trashed-out culture of ours
Approaching the wall, plants and animals
Disappearing at warp speed
Soil turned to dust, aquifers drained dry
And I see it's too painful to go there

It's too painful to go there
I'm headed outside for a smoke
It's too painful to go there
I'm busy learning Italian
It's too painful to go there
My therapist told me to stay positive
She said whatever I experience is up to me
That I create my own reality
My guru said the same thing

But it's funny, no matter what they say
I keep seeing this weirdness out of
The corner of my eye, I see undercover agents
On every transport platform watching over

My fellow Americans strapped into bucket seats
I see my fellow Americans weighed down
By schedules and cell phones
And computers and wristwatches
I see their children swallowing pharmaceuticals
To get through the day
While in nearby fields the birds and animals
Look on with infinite patience, waiting outside
Of clock time for us to burn out and disappear
(The yellow-throated warbler singing
"Is that the best you can do? Best you can do?"
"Is that the best you can do?")

I hear something
I hear the siren song of nationalism
Driving us onto the rocks
9/11 and the war in Iraq
No more than red herrings
Distracting us from this fact
Because Iraqis are people just like us
How can their deaths be worth less than ours

I see it's time for us to take a look in the mirror
Notice the frightened children in there
Wondering how they got into this mess
Realize there's no one in the whole wide world
To blame, decide to risk everything
And open our hearts, the one thing
Against which the rotund bastard has no defense

If you see something, say something
I see that even though my therapist charges
A hundred and seventy-five an hour and my guru
Has a lifetime free pass, maybe they're right
I'm responsible for what's happening to me
My beliefs create my experience
Otherwise why am I swallowed up

In rituals of mutual self-destruction while
Outside a sweet wind blows through the trees

Because I see two wolves fighting in my heart
One vengeful and the other compassionate
Which one will I feed today
Will I come after you, blaming and accusing
Or will I behave as if
The god in all of life matters
Which one will I feed today

9/11 – A TRUE STORY

Despite the unease it still causes me
I need to mention that twelve or
Thirteen years ago I had dinner
With a woman I hardly knew
But we warmed to each other
And toward the end of the meal
She told me in a heartfelt manner
To which I can't begin to do justice
Something confided to her
By a woman friend of hers
A "psychic on the run," as she put it
On the run from the government
Something to do with the C.I.A.
And her story brings tears to my eyes
Even years later when I recall it

The psychic related to my new friend
She had more than a vision, rather
A retro-cognition, a full-on visitation
That the perpetrators of 9/11
After crashing that plane
Into the World Trade Center
And incinerating
Were completely involved in the moment
Helping across those who were dying
Taking them by the hand
Ushering them into the light

I can't remember whether she said
They apologized for what they'd done
But in any case this was bigger
And more immediate than that
After their psychotic mindsets went up
In flames along with their robot bodies

They were no longer
Crazed adherents of anything
They were simply being of service
As I said, I'm not doing this justice
And I have no judgment to make
This concerns only what took place
After they passed over

Since then I've gone back to my notebook
Trying to make sense of what I was told
But there's not much more to relate
Because even at the time I felt like
I wasn't taking in the whole story
I was so blown away by it

And the very last thing
The psychic said to my friend
From an undisclosed location
Just before a black helicopter
Swooped down to carry her away
Never to be heard from again
Was that sooner or later
A shadow falls across the wall
The cards are dealt face up
Everyone a victim
Windblown and forsaken
No matter what they say
No matter what they do
"Shine like the sun
While you can," she said
Her voice faint and crackling
Over the phone
"Shine like a million suns"

WHO'S A TERRORIST

How can those who
continue to exterminate
indigenous people and
erase forests and jungles
around this kidnapped world
be called anything
but terrorists

And were the cruel fantasies
which for centuries dictated
the murderous behavior
of missionaries and colonists
any less insane than those
inside the frozen minds
of today's suicide bombers

Why do we insist on
defining as terrorists
only those intent on doing
us harm today while many
of us follow in a direct
line from ancestors who
essentially did the same

SAY GOODBYE

for Ai Wei Wei

This poem is dedicated to the millions of children
on the march yesterday, today and tomorrow
refugees drowning in the alphabet soup of nation-states
running from country to country, their lives a mash-up
of violence and fear, but our turn is coming soon
right here in the good old US of A, so pack your bags
and say goodbye to the upper middle class palace
you've been guarding nonstop or else coveting enviously
cause the big wave's rolling in for real and it ain't
gonna spare Pittsburgh and the only way to survive
will be to travel light on every level

Your time as refugee is just around the bend
and you'll be out on the road with nothing more
than you can carry, out on the road called all sorts
of names by those lucky few ignored for maybe
another week or two, they're still living in their
gimcrack apartments, their lights and water on
and they're leaning out of windows calling you
freeloader and vermin and rapist and terrorist
you who are just trying to keep from croaking
from one day to the next

So you better say goodbye to your carefully nurtured
career and obsessive plans for your children's success
say goodbye to your dear friends and detested enemies
to your favorite vacation spots, your cherished barking
and chirping pets, say goodbye to your bank cards and
your as yet undelivered driverless car, say goodbye
to the movie of the week and the lover of the month
and to your mailbox by the side of the road waiting
for the letters that will never arrive, and be sure
to say a special goodbye in advance to your impressive

obituary on the front page of the New York Times

Say goodbye to your treasured tableware and stunning
outfits and your furniture and potted plants and say
goodbye to Zumba classes and foodie extravaganzas
and little packets of heroin and pillboxes of pain killers
and don't forget the Thanksgiving dinners you won't
be able to eat and the piles of Christmas presents
you'll have to abandon, and how can you not say
goodbye to your Easter bunny all covered in chocolate
even though he's hopping disconsolately down
the muddy track in the rain trying to keep up with you
as you trudge off to nowhere with a big smile on your face
which until this very moment would have been seen as
perfectly insane but is now your most precious possession
the only proof you have that you're still alive

INTERSPECIES COMMUNICATION

Through the ultimate union of force and finesse
In order to ensure regular periods of grieving
For our dying companions, we masters insist
On a counter-intuitive diet for our animal friends
Who, no matter how deeply domesticated
Originated in the wild eating raw meat

We make sure they eat dead, denatured food
From cans and dry pouches, over the years
Watching as they become obese and tumor-ridden
Which no matter how much we suffer along
With them, is somehow reassuring because
That's basically where we too are headed

All the while our canine and feline playmates
For the most part stare at us reproachfully
Unable or unwilling to communicate what they
Actually need, so intent are these faithful escorts
On pleasing their masters, knowing they're the latest
In a long line of human and non-human pets

Sometimes they manage to give us looks of complicity
And heroic resignation, loving us wholeheartedly
In spite of being fed a diet that's slowly killing them
And in spite of us doing the same to ourselves
On rare occasions they even peer far into our eyes
As if to say, "We accept but do not understand you"

SPARKY NEEDS A NEW HOME

Sparky needs a new home because
his previous owner claims he or she
lost his or her job and apartment
and laid Sparky on me yesterday
without any warning or apology
which may be what I deserve for
trusting a paramour or husband or
partner or wife too much when you
can't even tell what sex this person
is anymore much less if they really still
care about you when the lights go out

But Sparky's a joy to be around
he's a full-on people dog who can
run and play with a playmate
and also pretty much ignore other
dogs if need be, in other words
he's versatile and very *very* friendly
a purebred English pointer who's
been gun trained and done plenty
of bird hunting although his most
recent household included five
children and an adorable tabby cat
who are also searching for a home

And I'm sorry about the crummy
cell phone photos where he looks
totally bug-eyed and stressed
he was just in the car for four hours
and then got busy meeting three
new dogs but he's calmed down
a bit already on his first evening here
in this nameless strip mall or suburb
or wherever we are at this point in time

Sparky is a special guy, though, so his
new owner also needs to be special
no punks or drug takers or blowhard
Fox News junkies, no unbalanced types
or watchers of internet sex with animals
just somebody with a big heart and
enough money so the hound can eat
the choicest possible food regularly
be given unhurried massages in a
smoke and chemical free environment
and not be left behind if the new owner
decides on a moment's notice to
take off to the Bahamas or Australia
or loses his or her mind completely
late one night, swallowing dozens of pills
in a brazen but futile attempt to end it all
while Sparky's in a corner trying to sleep

Because if that's the situation forget it
I won't give him up even though
I myself have no room for him
and would otherwise have to consider
euthanasia or some such execrable fate
for this loving and happy neutered male
seven years old and about 55 pounds
very fit, very active but not nuts
just in case you know of someone
willing to adopt him and the five quiet
and extremely well-behaved children
with their somewhat pudgy tabby cat

WHITE PEOPLE TRYING TO GET LOOSE

After having seen the light in India
in the late '80s, I returned to America
and found myself in the Boston area
not knowing what else to do
I opened a yoga studio in Cambridge
even though, to tell the truth
my grasp of the asanas remained
scarcely more than adequate
but once I employed the right teachers
young and limber and energetic
with that pranic glow in their eyes
I was free to teach the one thing
I thought I'd be good at, a class
devoted not to yoga per se but to
white people trying to get loose
utilizing techniques I'd learned in India
from Osho and other swamis who
were mapping the way to total freedom
but soon I discovered I'd bitten off
considerably more than I could chew
such an undertaking proving anything
but simple or straightforward
given the shifting multi-faceted rigidity
with which my students had been
boxed in by the dominator culture
and I discovered that the more I guided
everyone into physical, emotional
and sexual release, the more full-throated
bellowing of all the raging sound
and fury bound up in clueless bodies
led to an avalanche of trouble I had
not foreseen and could not handle
so that by the time two years passed
I was utterly worn out from acting as

teacher and guru and orgasmic tag-team
facilitator, not to mention engaging in
psychic battles with whoever felt left out
to the point that one frigid winter morning
I collapsed and decided to close the studio
finally being reborn the following summer
as a realtor in the burgeoning Boston area
housing market and then, marrying a go-getter
public relations whiz, I fell into co-ownership
of a rambling split level in one of the
far-flung suburbs, becoming somebody
I'd never considered remotely possible before
the father of one, then two, then three
awesome and oh so demanding boys
whose own version of getting loose
erupted a decade later in a swirling tornado
of alcohol, Prozac, Adderal, cold pizza
and never-ending, costly visits to the child
psychiatrist with whom my indomitable wife
was having the most explosive affair ever
in her otherwise highly disciplined life
while as for me—as for me—I…

MOST PEDICURES START OUT THIS WAY

Most pedicures start out this way
rudely plunging into a frenzy
of clipping and sanding and veneer
without so much as a howdy do
but a pedicurist to the stars says
this will only mask your problems
because although it's certainly true
that your toenails are itsy teeny tiny
in relation to your body as a whole
not to mention your so-called mind
they are also symphonic and real
and must be approached with the
respect accorded to a dangerous animal
encountered in the bush, or else your
nightmare of a melting orchestra
will come to pass due to your reckless
disregard for the boundaries of things
as your body teeters on the dissolving
lip of the unknown and you realize
that even though you're carried away
by your newfound celebrity, finally
starring in the movie of your dreams
said movie unwinds in all directions
and your only recourse is to cry out
the name of the pedicurist to the stars
begging her to make it known
to your nethermost parts how much
you admire and need them because
if your body tries to keep its balance
in its present fragmentary state
who can say where in our roiling
black hole of climate change and
funny money and stage names
you and your dizzying toenails

of lime green and electric blue
will end up as you search feverishly
for a place of stability and refuge

THERE'S A REASON WE CARE DEEPLY

There's a reason we care deeply
that the drink we prepare for you
is nothing less than perfect, because
your psychological state at home
and at work has passed our rigorous
inspection with flying colors and
therefore we have no hesitation
in welcoming you with open arms
and paper party hats, so to speak
—here's looking at you!

This holds true even though
a troubling vein in your behavior
continues to draw our scrutiny
namely your late night dreams
filled with outrageous episodes
of uncontrolled libertinage
including what cannot be called
anything but a shameless indulgence
in sex with borderline adolescents
both male and female, and we wonder
if these hallucinations are more real
to you than your waking life since
once you're seated at the breakfast table
the only memory you have of them
if it can be called memory at all
is a certain vague but potent undertow
which never stops pulling at you
as you go about your daily rounds
—bottoms up!

But in spite of these nightly escapades
in the end we feel quite comfortable
turning a blind eye to your fantasy life

we accept you for what you are
and as long as we can count on you
to carry on putting up no resistance
to the goofball brainwash of your
official identity as a typical tax-paying
citizen, we are more than happy
to fix that perfect drink for you
and fix it for you again and again
until the end of your days
—prosit!

LIFE AT THE TOP

Life at the top is pretty darn good
Blue skies and tables by the window
La Chinita serving you with a naked
Smile, La Chinita the girl you always
Wanted, half Chinese and half Latina
Fifteen years old at the very most
Jailbait for anyone with less pull than you
For anyone with less payback due
But for you nothing's too much
So it's time to stop fucking around
Get exactly what you want and
To hell with the rest, no turning back
Just full steam ahead, lovely La Chinita
Day and night at your beck and call
Serving you the last of the planet's
Culinary tidbits, the last pure water
The last fresh air, La Chinita making
Every dream of yours come true
Including as a fitting climax to your life
The grand finale of your very own design
A little push she gives you from behind
Your swan dive from the sixty-fifth floor
After you've seen there's no denying
The poles are melting, the so-called
World order crumbling before your eyes
Dollar bills worth no more than rags
While at home your rancid sausage
Of a wife stands waiting, meat cleaver
In hand, to separate your swollen head
From your shoulders and from here on
Partner, there can be no way out but down

IF I WERE YOU

If I were you which in many ways
of course I already am, I'd wipe
that big smile off our face and
stop telling everybody how great
we feel while deep down inside
we're inconsolable over our dearly
departed Earth Mommy falling
without warning into an unmarked
open mineshaft while before Dad
even heard the telltale splash he
ran off in search of someone new
some magnetizing little cutie with
a stainless steel butt and no memories

When Tycoon Daddy thought he had
located that person, she was holding
the key to eternal youth in her hand
a key she painlessly inserted into his
left ear and with a brisk half-turn
to the right erased what remained of
his once formidable common sense
so that with a serene yet senile smile
on his face this perennial poster man
for global capitalism proceeded
to the nearest branch of the bank
of which he was majority owner
and withdrew the lion's share
of his vast fortune in the form of a
cashier's check made out to what's
her name, who immediately pulled
the key out of his ear and disappeared
leaving only the tough synthetic scent
of her timeless body to torture Dad

In no time at all she had resurfaced
on the stage set of a reality TV show
starring the 100-year-old surfer boy
she'd had her eye on forever and
waiting for a break in the action
she laid the cashier's check at his feet
all of this having direct repercussions
for you and me because as I said before
I can no longer separate myself from you
or from your fate in any meaningful way
so we're both hard at work assembling
burgers at Wendy's from dawn till dusk
whereupon we wend our way back to
the abandoned railroad car we call home
turn our heads to the wall and try
to catch a few hours of sleep before
the alarm clock rings at 5:45 a.m. and
once again we fix our pre-diabetic kids
Froot Loops with growth-hormone milk
hoping they'll be alright alone, that is to say
with countless others exactly like them
as we depart for another day and another
fifty-eight dollars and thirty-two cents
still dreaming of what might have been
if Mom hadn't dropped like a stone
into oblivion and Dad, blind as a bat
hadn't followed suit in his inimitable fashion

PLEASE DON'T CRITICIZE

I know plenty about
how it's not good for me
but I can't help myself
late at night while
the rest of the town
supposedly is asleep
I don my queen-size
white polyester sheet
with two small holes
cut out so I can see
and float through
the dark silent streets
past the town limits
joining the other ghosts
my comrades in arms
we disappear head first
into metal dumpsters
behind the big box store
for a late night indulgence
we're here to eat the plastic
in every shape and form
and please don't criticize
after all I'm pretty smart
I'm perfectly aware of
what keeps me returning
night after night, it's
that crazy group mind thing
we're all in this together
have been for years
and during our lunch hour
when we spot each other
at McDonald's takeout window
or sneaking off for another visit
to the Museum of Plastic

in the basement of City Hall
we smile conspiratorially
as we pull out and suck on
pieces of vintage food wrap
left over from our sandwiches
little shreds of plastic saturated
with the memory of what we live for
after our long workday is done

TO A HALIBUT

I know you're not sexy
You don't belong to an endangered species
And I've been told that in mid-summer
When you're most abundant
In your habitual deepwater haunts
Your body is filled with worms
And your mind is filled with consternation
And that this has been going on for
Who knows how long, although in
Recent times the worms have been joined
By plastic pellets the size of your usual diet
Namely anything that fits into your mouth
So I wouldn't dream of eating you
Even if I wanted to
But – halibut – I still love you

BOTTLED WATER BLUES

17 million barrels of oil per year
to make all plastic water bottles
in the US alone, enough oil
to fuel 1.3 million cars for a year

Three times more water to make
a bottle of water than to fill it

Imagine a water bottle filled
with one-quarter oil, the amount
of fossil fuel needed to make it

Then see a fleet of 40,000 18-wheelers
to deliver the water every week

Water bottles are polyethylene
terephthalate (PET) plastics
PETs don't biodegrade they
photodegrade, break down
into small fragments over time

Fragments that absorb toxins
polluting waterways, contaminating soil
and sickening the animals we then eat

National recycle rate for PETs
only 23 percent, meaning we
throw 38 billion water bottles
into landfills every year

38 billion environmentally
poisonous time bombs
taking centuries to decompose

Hormone-disrupting phthalates
leach into bottled water after
as little as ten weeks of storage
much faster if bottles are left
in the sun (like in the car)

Chemicals used in food contact materials
(wrappers, cans, and bottles) contain
formaldehyde, a cancer-causing agent
as well as tribytyltin, triclosan, phthalates
and BPA, an endocrine disruptor
linked to hormonal damage and cancer

Found in many plastics including baby bottles
aluminum can linings, register receipts
BPA is banned in Europe

Cognitive dissonance
Why are we doing this
How do we put on the brakes

80-year-old activist Jean Hill of Concord, Massachusetts,
the first town in the US to ban plastic water bottles: "The
bottled water companies are draining our aquifers and
selling the water back to us. I'm going to work until I
drop on this."

A VAST POOL OF SELTZER

No ice-free Arctic for
the last three million years

Once summer sea ice loss
passes the point of no return
methane feedbacks kick in
methane 105 times more potent
than carbon dioxide when it
comes to heating the planet

Offshore permafrost sea beds
warming and melting
great plumes of methane
in the Siberian Sea
a vast pool of seltzer bubbling
as far as the eye can see

In a single year vents only
30 centimeters across
grew to one kilometer wide
with non-linear rapidity

Climate transformation from
full-scale permafrost melt
not reversible during our lifetimes
possibly bringing our extinction
say during the next few decades

We've never lived on a planet
at 3.5 degrees Celsius above baseline
some estimates predict six or seven C
temperature increases by the year 2100

If global temperature spikes

by four to six degrees
ocean plankton is destroyed
removing habitat for humans
and yes the human body could
handle a six to nine degree C
rise in planetary temperature
but crops we use for food cannot

Cognitive dissonance
Why are we doing this
How do we put on the brakes

The only way the United Nations
Climate Change Convention
can achieve even a 2-degree goal is
to say goodbye to capitalism and
re-vision the entire global economy

Re-visioning the global economy: let's not be naïve and assume
that those whose greed drives the way things work are
unaware of what's coming. They see climate change leading to
war and famine and are making plans for their survival at the
expense of others. So changing their perception, literally
changing what they see—that's re-visioning.

And changing what they see for the most part starts not with
them but with their children. Via actual human contact.
Which those whose greed drives the way things work will do
their utmost to prevent. So re-visioning is risky. It takes place
in real time. It's whoever walks up to these children, looks
them in the eye and says, "You and I both know what's going
on. We don't need it."

FOR THEM

Running, biking
skiing, golfing
throwing, catching
biting, sucking
kicking, screaming
texting, snapping
that's how they know they're alive

And for them
to keep them busy
full of energy
hydrated and well-fed
with a positive outlook
their cars filled with gasoline
for them we cut down the world

CANDY CRUSH SAGA

Candy Crush Saga
the hugely popular
digital puzzle game
has 97 million users
every day trying
to line up three pieces
of matching virtual sugar

The state's security forces
are forever bowing
to a political ideology
when their duty
should be to protect
the people out there
playing video games

THE INTERNET OF THINGS

As the Internet of Things matures
appliances and physical objects
will become more networked
your ceiling lights and thermostat
your television and washing machine
even your socks will be wired
to interact online and the F.B.I.
will not have to bug your living room
you'll do it yourself, although in point
of fact the Internet of Things goes
beyond the F.B.I. snooping on you
and it's not only about corporate
capitalism tracking what to sell you
even before you know you want it
because ultimately the Internet of Things
refers to the checkmate made on your
personal space when it comes time to decide
who will be sacrificed and who will be spared
as the rivers run dry and the storerooms
filled with grain are emptied down to their
rat shit covered floors and the last precious
piece of information you're allowed
to carry with you as you make your exit
is the secret to perfectly cooked salmon
which not that long ago the Internet of Things
bestowed on you in a moment of sheer generosity
seeming to come out of nowhere and easily
winning you over to its agenda of convenience

WHENEVER WE DESIGN OR DISCUSS WEBSITES

Whenever we design
or discuss websites
we invent
rock-solid
but non-existent
purely conceptual
structures

Metaphors
accepted
by consensus
just as money
is money
because people
believe in it

Nothing supporting
the billowing
safety net
of our beliefs
except habitual patterns
whose purpose is to
prevent our fall

Back into our bodies
our sweet bodies
ignored by technophoria
in its rush
to extend itself
all along the timeline
of a weightless arena

Filled with

seven billion or so
worldwide channels
operating simultaneously
but also
secretly
(touch me, hold me, taste me)

CHINESE INTERNET TRAFFIC

Chinese internet traffic
is redirected to a
building in Wyoming

A million jars
of peanut butter are
dumped in New Mexico

The huge electronic
screen commands us
GET ENERGIZED

TOO BUSY TO TALK

What is said and done online
never actually goes away
it's conserved as an integral part
of the information cloud itself
because at the highest level
there is no delete button
in spite of what we think
while we're skating on the surface
and in spite of our underlying
assumption that a fresh start
that wiping the slate clean
is our inalienable right
as lively networking people

But since our personal calendars
are so crammed with tasks
and appointments and plans
that we're too busy to talk
and we have to get back to you
later, maybe in the next lifetime
information is not properly digested
and the traces left on the glass
of our screens and pads and phones
become indelible, forever open
to inspection from above
no matter how much we remain
convinced of their ephemeral nature
no matter how certain we are
that what we say and do online
is erased with a simple keystroke

If for whatever reason
the cloud needs assistance
from below, from the incarnate

realm of hard drives and memory
the contents of our deleted files
can be relayed back to agents
and analysts on the ground
who specialize in retrieval for
the purpose of creating enough static
while we're searching for a signal
buried somewhere in the noise
that soon we are even more
too busy to talk than before

Because of these disturbances
we have great trouble sensing
the cloud enveloping us although
we're aware just under the skin
of a nervous tingling or vibration
this is what information feels like
when it never goes away
when the cloud is working its magic
leaving us more and more agitated
until presently we see mouths moving
we hear the people around us talking
or even shouting at the top of their lungs
in this most real and vivid of dreams
which we invent and then forget
split second after split second
for the ongoing gratification of the cloud

NO OVERLAY

Nothing laid over naked awareness
No Christian overlay, no Jewish overlay
No Hindu overlay, no Moslem overlay
No Buddhist overlay, no atheist overlay
No capitalist overlay, no communist overlay
No Democratic overlay, no Republican overlay
No conspiracy theory overlay, no sentimental overlay
No literary overlay, no Hollywood overlay
No military overlay, no art world overlay
No psychoanalytic overlay, no neurotic overlay
No corporate overlay, no snowmobile overlay
No boot camp overlay, no patriotic overlay
No IRS overlay, no libertarian overlay
No manic overlay, no depths-of-despair overlay
No family values overlay, no strip mall overlay
No Fox News overlay, no New Yorker overlay
No UFO overlay, no Botox overlay
No invasive species overlay, no smartphone overlay
No Darwinian overlay, no creationist overlay
No karmic overlay, no shit happens overlay
No alcoholic overlay, no sober-as-a-judge overlay
No creative writing overlay, no divinity school overlay
No vow of silence overlay, no rock star overlay
No gangsta overlay, no New Age overlay
No pharmaceutical overlay, no Monsanto overlay
No non-violent overlay, no huntin' and fishin' overlay
No vegan overlay, no Big Mac overlay
No apocalyptic overlay, no head-in-the-sand overlay
Simply being present
Like this grove of Eastern white pines
Sixty to a hundred feet tall
On Mount Desert Island
Midway up the coast of Maine
On a completely clear, completely still
Summer afternoon
Just as it is

PLANETARY PATRIOTS

(Washington D.C., 2007)

These people call themselves Christians but they aren't
They would've killed Jesus in a heartbeat
They call themselves patriots but they aren't
Patriots act for the good of their country
Instead of sucking it dry out of greed
Then dragging the rest of the world down with it

And, I'm sorry, but you know who they are
You know their names, their faces, their "constituency"
You know they inhabit the high places
Drive around in motorcades
Wave at crowds from behind bulletproof glass
You know they call themselves freedom-loving
But they act like tyrants
And you realize that deep down
They know not what they do
But since you're not Jesus, you can't help it
You hold that fact against them

These people call themselves Americans, but they aren't
They belong to no place and exist in no time
They think in agendas, they feel in prescribed allotments
They call themselves peace-loving
While talking of collateral damage
They wonder why the rest of the world hates them
Even though they're honorable and God-fearing
Even though they brake for animals
And support no smoking in public places

And they beat the fake drum of exceptionalism
Insisting America is destined for eternal greatness
They find it maddening when others believe the opposite
Or believe nothing at all – in fact, just like they do

Although they'd be the last to admit it

Because the largest state in America is the state of denial
It runs from leaking Alaskan oilfields
Down to the dying coral reefs of Key West
In the state of denial, new prisons outnumber new schools
In the state of denial, climate change is an inconvenience
In the state of denial, "free trade" is forced on other people
While our own corporations are protected
Out of fear we make enemies everywhere
Defending ourselves against them
With ever-larger military expenditures
Soon we'll declare war against the entire planet
Then blame the Armageddon to come
On a fundamentalist monster
A monster we ourselves have created

America, Jesus still loves you no matter what you do
He forgives your sins
He wipes away your tears
And invites you to visit him in Jerusalem
You watch while he chases
The money-changers from the Temple
You witness him heal the halt and the blind
But you turn a deaf ear when he says
The meek shall inherit the earth

Instead you climb into armored helicopters
And fly away, covering your escape
With bullets of depleted uranium
Convinced you're making the homeland secure
For your children and your children's children
Forgetting that you can no longer afford
To destroy the world out of righteousness
You can no longer be patriots of one country
At the expense of all others

111

Because like it or not, we're all planetary patriots now
Everyone our brothers and sisters
As Jesus himself would tell you if you'd listen

ONE WORD IS WORTH A THOUSAND PICTURES

One word is worth a thousand pictures
Here's a word
"Love"
That's worth a thousand pictures
And two words worth at least two thousand pictures
"Love me"
And here are four words worth four thousand pictures
 "L'enfer c'est les autres"
Jean-Paul Sartre said that
It's French for "Hell is other people"

Then one night the ghost of Antonin Artaud
Came and took Sartre by the hand
And led him into the jungles of Peru
This must have been sometime in 1952
After days of fasting naked in the forest
He was fed great doses of ayahuasca, the vision vine
Whereupon the distinguished philosopher
A big, beaming smile on his face
Announced, "Heaven is other people"

But when he returned to Paris
Dressed once again in existential black
He realized he had a persona to uphold
So Sartre never divulged what had taken place
Deep in the jungles of Peru
And as the years went by he forgot all about it
Except for two little words worth two thousand pictures
Which he cried out in the middle of the night
"Love me!"

LET'S GET LOST

Global Positioning System says
We always know your coordinates
But better than that we have
No real need to know where you are
Because you do the job for us
Inner surveillance
Self-tracking mechanism
Fail-safe and worry-free

But I say
Let's get lost
Melt down our inner GPS devices
And disappear
For the longest lost weekend on record
Lasting the rest of our lives
Let's say goodbye
To those seen-it-all eyes in the mirror
Like a clueless guest
They've overstayed their welcome
Let's say goodbye
To hustling back and forth
Between point A and point B
Believing we don't deserve better
Let's say goodbye
To same-as-yesterday jobs
Airtight families
Trance-inducing television
To the news we've all heard
A thousand times before
Let's say goodbye
To cascading boredom

Boredom which guarantees
That even if we get rowdy

Even if we get loaded
Even if we get high
And leap out of rockets
Onto the far side of the moon
Even if we change our names
And re-enter the game
Dyed hair
Plastic surgery
A fake passport
It'll never be enough
Those same eyes
Keeping track of us
In the mirror

Instead, the best medicine
The only medicine
Drop the whole thing
Don't look back
We'll drown our wristwatches
Enter a virginal landscape
No idea what time it is
Cruising the blissful unknown
Safe in each other's company
Not insisting on who we are
Like grown-up versions
Of the children we once were
The children who were stolen from us

SOME CHILDREN

Some children
a long, long time ago
(a day, a week, a month ago)
like heroes broke out of
the chain mail armor fastened
tightly around their bodies

they ran into an open meadow
carpeted with wildflowers
where they encountered ancient trees
and listened to the empty calls
of an owl who soon became
their friend and teacher

the owl told them never to
enter the field of mortal combat
being prepared for them but instead
to abandon whoever they were
being groomed to impersonate during
their time on this earth as grown-ups

the children listened intently to the owl
they bared their hearts to the heavens
and cried out, "We're free!"
then for the first time they noticed
a large collection of unhappy faces
gathered along the meadow's edge

this legion of depressed adults was being
given a once-in-a-lifetime chance to join
the children but never on any account
scheme to own them, because love isn't
possible without freedom and the sad sacks
would only be free by somehow

or other becoming indistinguishable
from the children themselves, who now
invited the adults to follow them
into cities teeming with scary crowds
and join them as they smiled fearlessly
day after day into guarded eyes

have you met any of these kids yet
a day, a week, a month ago
and when you do will you coat them
with your profiteering projections
thereby going unconscious
or will you fall to your knees

yes, fall to your knees on the most
insanely crowded sidewalk in the city
people endlessly pushing past you
to someplace else, people just not seeing
these kids for who they really are
emissaries from a meadow free of combat

SLIPPING THE LEASH

Finally I get it
The political is personal
Slipping the leash
How to break free
Nothing else matters
Time staring me in the face
Battles, alliances, betrayals
Political parties, systems, strategies
Right and wrong, left and right
Turn my back on all that
Drop the entire seductive arena
Like dog shit wrapped in brocade
Because the push and pull never ends
There's no gyroscope in samsara
And maybe I've been of service
Tilting at clowns and criminals
But there's more to deal with now
How to be of service to myself

Been straining at the leash
For decades
Only to discover
The leash is internal
Look in the mirror
Who's looking back at me
Still don't know
"Michael Brownstein"
Identity inside quotation marks
Product of cultural conditioning
Peer pressure and consensus reality
Even when I thought otherwise
Rarely autonomous
Endless stories I told myself
Status, relationships, money, health

How to break free
Cut the tie that binds
Recycle the self-image
I've carried around all these years
Like the world's heaviest book
With everyone's name
Inscribed in it but mine

Yes, the political is personal
Which doesn't mean it's not also political
Doesn't mean there aren't dark forces
But instead of resisting them
Redefine myself in relation to them
No other choice really
Time staring me in the face
The only question
How do I slip the leash
Drop what hasn't served me
No praise, no blame
Move from slavery to freedom
From other-directed to spacious
Move beyond ownership
Beyond self-imposed limitations
But this time without fighting
Without enemies
Unarmored and open
The way everyone secretly wants to be

Because up till now
I've been good at making enemies
Another kind of armor
Judging, blaming, accusing
Myself as well as others
Myself more than others
Instead how do I embody
The stillness at the center
Wu wei

Doing nothing, having everything
How do I break free
Entanglements, longings, rage
Fantasies, disappointments
Pulling me along by the neck
How do I come home to myself
Simply arriving

The only answer
What unites me with others
Not what divides us
And why not
If we can visualize it
We can do it
Look at all the pernicious junk
We've thought of so far
Everyone said we couldn't fly
And look, we've filled the sky
With unmanned drones
Obliterating nameless farmers
Halfway around the world
And everyone said
We couldn't map the genome
But look, a chicken with rhinoceros skin
Able to live and breed underwater
So let's figure out how to pick
The lock of separation
Transcend our suspicions
Person to person
Every last one of us
Embrace baseline human
The light filling the universe fills us
As soon as we're aware of it
As soon as we're empty enough
To see it, love it, work it
Leaving behind business as usual
The airtight realm of distraction

Noisy tapes of personal history
Whirring inside our heads
Defining who we are
Trances people live
Far from our unarmored selves
Far from essence

And tell me what love is
When it's deeper than our names
Out past our laboring personas
Where we're free
Not beyond people
I didn't say that
You and me
We're still here
How could we not be
But beyond our stories
Who would you be without your story
The courage to do this
And land somewhere beyond
The interminable tall tale
We keep telling ourselves
To prove that we exist
Prove that we own
Whatever love comes our way
Put it in a little box
Swallow it
Now it's mine
But that's the catch
It's not mine
Real love radiates
Out beyond ownership

So it all starts with me
Make friends with naked awareness
No more other-directed, no more
Group mind, fatalistic and cynical

No more swimming back and forth
In a materialistic fish tank
Bumping up against the glass
Telling myself this is all there is

Not surprising the lottery's everywhere
These days—Power Ball, Mega Millions
People want out
Jackpot, breakthrough
Every month the same bills
Family to support
Image to live up to
Trouble in mind
Each year more difficult
To feel at ease, feel secure while
The hunter-gatherers we're descended from
Could they even have imagined a lottery
Much less wanted one
To win what

Question: Why won't the hamster jump off the wheel
Answer: Because it's moving too fast

I make a vow
No longer define myself by what I do
No expectations, no fixed address
Release as best I can whatever freezes me
Fear of poverty
Fear of sick and old
Lonely and decrepit
Fear of dying
I've been soaking in a brainwash
Of negative anticipation
Up till now
Tethered to fear
Like a lapdog afraid of the forest
Out beyond the backyard

Even if the leash came undone
I'd return to the kitchen door
To the warm light in the window
Begging for canned food
My tail between my legs

So no fixed address
That's the first thing
Abandon my fear of being adrift
Of not having a home
Don't have one anyway
Tried that once and it didn't work
Bought the wrong place
With money I didn't have
Learned the hard way
What it comes down to
Am I brave enough
Step into the unknown
Drop the fake certainty
I've been fed all these years
The certainty which isn't certain
The certainty which doesn't exist
Just as I exist only provisionally
Smoke and mirrors, three card monte
Identity a shell game
We keep rearranging the pieces
Generation after generation
Lifetime after lifetime
Not remembering any of it
Buddhists call this dependent origination
Whatever arises takes on its identity
In relation to something else
Which in turn arises
Depending on something else
Impossible to pin any of it down
That would include me too

I take a deep breath
Let go of certainty
Follow my instinct
After all
What am I holding onto
With such desperation
This physical body
Aching, creaky, full of surprises
Not all of them pleasant
But do I live my life
Through this body
Or is life larger than that
I have a body but I am not this body
Because I've already experienced
The light surrounding this
Comfort zone we call our lives
Luminous and never-ending
An active, loving, brilliant energy
When my time comes I'll go there
And even now, if I wish
Via sacred plant medicines
Emissaries from the beyond
Catapulting me into a realm
Outside knee-jerk identity
Who I am without my programs running
Glorious universe off the leash
So why am I sometimes still afraid

Shining examples
Of how to proceed with this
Celebratory cultures long gone
And shamans, yogis, warriors of today
Some appearing anonymously
Without cultural markers of any kind
No indigenous paraphernalia
Just that look in their eyes
Saying once I slip the leash

Nothing can harm me
On the contrary I'll be free
And search for others of like mind
I'll know I've found them
When suddenly things get playful
Trusting the human circle again
Making friends with inner space
What I have is yours

No more the workaday tunesmith
Obligated every morning
To come up with a new tune
Like all the other tunesmiths
Running to keep up
Tunes for an amnesiac culture
Tunes for Gringostan's entertainment
Pouring our creations into a hole
Wearing us down
No matter how big the paycheck
No matter how we wrack our brains
To make our tunes clever and bright
Till the time comes to wheel us out

But things could be different
Throw away our straight lines
Join the circle again
Original humanity
Together on the beach
Eyes wide with pleasure
Yes we deserve it
Yes we can do it
Dancing right out of our leashes
The same songs all night long
Sacred refrains, sacred repetition
Because now the songs aren't for sale
They belong to no one
They're songs for everyone

Sweet revelation, weight lifted
We're not chained
To claustrophobic stories anymore
He did this to me, she said that
Who would you be without your story
Who indeed
How refreshing
No longer ducking from the past
Or chasing the future
But going from never enough time
To all the time in the world
So yes you could say
It's tribal identification we want
But without romanticizing it
21st century tribal
When written history just stops
Which maybe terrifies us
But that's where we're headed
Smoked out of our hiding places
Like it or not here we come
Breaking free
Of deadly seriousness
Abandoning the rat race
Imposed on us
By life's dictators

And sooner or later we find one another
Everyone who's managed to slip the leash
Determined to live without money
Not even knowing yet what that means
Determined to live without competition
Without fear of coming up short
Members of the same species again
Like crows when they congregate
High up in the trees
Their voices change, a new register sounds

A new vocabulary, purring and gurgling
Sweetly conversing
Hundreds then thousands
Then millions of us
Physical, energetic, spiritual beings
Home at last, our lonely
Wanting, worrying, and wondering
A distant memory
As the sun rises in the morning sky
Flooding our faces with gold
And we turn to one another and laugh

AND NOW WE OPEN UP THE BIG ROOM

And now we open up the big room
we step inside to see for certain
what we could not see before
that after all no one can possibly
harm us in any way because
the big room is empty
except for floor to ceiling mirrors
and when we work up the nerve
to look into them, translucent
luminous figures gaze back at us
figures casting no shadows
but in spite of what we now know
we still can't stop ourselves
from counting on someone else
to appear who does cast a shadow

ONCE AGAIN DREAMLAND DRAWS NEAR

Once again dreamland draws near
the only question
will we remain conscious this time
staying anchored in our bodies
as we float along her winding green lanes
her broken, rutted deer paths
or will we drift off and lose our way
among heaps of blue and white cumulus clouds
leading us into a mirror image deep forest
filled with everybody and everything
where we wander for another world age

CITATIONS

IN THE TRIBE, THE CHIEF IS UNDER SURVEILLANCE

"Primitive societies are undivided societies: classless societies—no rich exploiters of the poor; societies not divided into the dominating and the dominated—no separate organs of power. Why are primitive societies Stateless? As complete, adult societies, primitive societies do not have a State because they refuse it. Chieftainship in primitive society is only the supposed, apparent place of power. Where is its real place? It is the social body itself that holds and exercises power as an undivided unity.

"It follows that this power is exercised over the institution from which the insidiousness of power could arise, chieftainship. In the tribe, the chief is under surveillance; society watches to make sure the taste for prestige does not become the desire for power. If the chief's desire for power becomes too obvious, the procedure put into effect is simple: they abandon him, indeed, even kill him.

"The example of primitive societies teaches us that division is not inherent in the social being, that in other words, the State is not eternal. Why has it emerged? What is designated here is indeed this fatal rupture which should never have happened, this irrational event which we moderns call the birth of the State.

"The enigmatic misfortune from which History originates has denatured man by instituting a division in society; freedom, though inseparable from man's first being, is banished from it. The sign and proof of this loss of freedom can be witnessed not only in the resignation to submission but in the love of servitude. Then the misfortune occurs: everything is turned upside down.

133

The result of this split between free society and slave society is that all divided societies are slave societies.

"Desire for submission, refusal of obedience: society with a State, society without a State. Primitive societies refuse power relations *by preventing the desire for submission from coming into being.* The desire for power cannot come into being unless it manages to evoke its necessary complement, the desire for submission. There is no realizable desire to command without the correlative desire to obey."

Pierre Clastres, *The Archeology of Violence*

GEORGE CATLIN ON THE PEOPLE HE PAINTED

"I love a people who have always made me feel welcome to the best they had, who were honest without laws, who had no jails, no poor houses, who keep the commandments without ever having read them or heard them preached from the pulpit, never swear, never take the name of God in vain, love their neighbor as themselves, free of religious animosity. I love a people who have never raised a hand against me, or stole my property, when there was no law to punish them for either. I love a people who have never fought a battle with white men except on their own ground. I love a people who live and keep what is their own without locks and keys. And oh, how I love a people who don't live for the love of money."

Manners, Customs, and Condition of the North
American Indians, 1841

ABRAHAM LINCOLN ON CORPORATIONS

"I see in the near future a crisis approaching that
unnerves me and causes me to tremble for the safety of
my country. As the result of the war, corporations have
been enthroned. An era of corruption in high places will
follow, and the money power of the country will
endeavor to prolong its reign by working upon the
prejudices of the people until wealth is aggregated in a
few hands...and the republic is destroyed."

from a letter of November 21, 1864

WHAT IS PATRIOTISM?

"What is patriotism? 'Patriotism, sir, is the last resort of scoundrels,' said Dr. Johnson. Leo Tolstoy, the greatest anti-patriot of our times, defines patriotism as the principle that will justify the training of wholesale murderers; a trade that requires better equipment for the exercise of man-killing than the making of such necessities of life as shoes, clothing, and houses; a trade that guarantees better returns and greater glory than that of the average worker.

"Indeed, conceit, arrogance, and egotism are the essentials of patriotism. Let me illustrate. Patriotism assumes that our globe is divided into little spots, each one surrounded by an iron gate. Those who have had the fortune of being born on some particular spot consider themselves better, nobler, grander, more intelligent than the living beings inhabiting any other spot. It is, therefore, the duty of everyone living on that chosen spot to fight, kill, and die in the attempt to impose his superiority upon all the others.

"The inhabitants of the other spots reason in like manner, of course, with the result that, from early infancy, the mind of the child is poisoned with blood-curdling stories about the Germans, the French, the Italians, the Russians, etc. When the child has reached manhood, he is thoroughly saturated with the belief that he is chosen by the Lord himself to defend his country against the attack or invasion of any foreigner. It is for that purpose that we are clamoring for a greater army and navy, more battleships and ammunition.

"We Americans claim to be a peace-loving people. Yet we go into spasms of joy over the possibility of projecting bombs from flying machines onto helpless citizens. Our hearts swell with pride at the thought that America is becoming the most powerful nation on earth, and that it will eventually plant her iron foot on the necks of all the other nations.

"When we have undermined the patriotic lie, we shall have cleared the path for that great structure wherein all nationalities shall be united into a universal brotherhood – a truly FREE SOCIETY."

Emma Goldman, *Patriotism: A Menace to Liberty* (1908)

THE ORIGINAL FORM OF POLLUTION

"It is obvious today that 'surviving' has so far prevented us from 'living'; that man's insistence on making himself useful in his work is actually of little use to him in his own life and even kills him.

"Economics has been the most durable lie of the approximately ten millennia mistakenly accepted as history. From it stem all those eternal truths and sacred causes that have governed master and slave alike, truths and causes to which generations, born simply to live, have been wantonly sacrificed.

"The time has come when the economic machine has begun to expose the cynical nakedness of its component parts. A long and bloody striptease has deprived it of myth and ideology. It no longer uses – nor needs – illusions and subterfuge to parody what it is and always has been: a system designed to ensure the survival of human beings at the expense of *living*.

"The first response to signs of beneficial change is neither *joie de vivre* nor creative release but fear – a fear so intense that a moribund economy can exploit it to keep a certain market active and well-supplied: it is the insecurity market, in which consumers must beg for strong-armed protection as they rush through the well-lit, clearly displayed aisles of consumable hedonism.

"The earliest legends, indelibly marked by nostalgia for a golden age and by hatred of women, admirably demonstrate what portion of real life the worshippers of the ithyphallic stone renounced and so fiercely repressed beneath the weight of the mind and the gods. By a reversal of perspective, the life force of the body was transformed into labor power.

"With the intrusion of work the body loses its sensual wholeness. It splits into two principles: the head, the controlling element, whose thought regulates and represses libidinal energy; and the body, the element that is controlled, reduced to a money-making musculature and menial hand.

"Once expelled from the body, the animality of passion reenters through the head. Market civilization does not transcend bestiality, it socializes it. It polices and urbanizes it in the rivalry of competition, greed for profit, legal and illegal appropriation, the survival of the fittest.

"From Sumerian conquests to concentration camps the ferocity of the animal world seems minor in comparison with the iron fist of power that lies inside the velvet glove of solidarity, justice, equality and love.

"Today the global disintegration of ecological equilibrium is completely tied up with the logic of an economy founded on dehumanization: as life expires beneath the growing exploitation that negates and turns it into survival, the preconditions of survival itself are threatened with destruction by the profit mechanism. The commodity is the original form of pollution."

Raoul Vaneigem, *The Movement of the Free Spirit*

HERMANN GOERING ON WAR

"Naturally the common people don't want war. But after all, it is the leaders of a country who determine the policy, and it's always a simple matter to drag people along whether it is a democracy or a fascist dictatorship, or a parliament, or a communist dictatorship. Voice or no voice, the people can always be brought to the bidding of the leaders. This is easy. All you have to do is tell them they are being attacked, and denounce the pacifists for lack of patriotism and for exposing the country to danger. It works the same in every country."

as told to Gustave Gilbert in Nuremberg Diary, 1947

GIANT POSTER OF MAO SEIZES POWER IN CHINA

Sunday, October 2, 1949

PEKING, China—

Ending a long and bitter civil war, the Chinese people today celebrated the transfer of power to a 15-foot by 20-foot poster of Communist Party Chairman Mao Tse-tung.

After the new poster-led government was established, a large rally was held in China's Tien An Men square, with the poster looking out approvingly over the crowd from atop a high balcony. Thousands came to pay tribute to the picture, which now leads the most populous nation on earth.

"We have put our faith in this great poster," said one Chinese citizen in attendance.

THE RISE OF THE POSTER

Not much is known in the West about the ruling poster, except that it is said to be made of the finest Chinese silk-bond cardboard stock.

Once a mere paper sign advertising the sale of pigs from a peasant farm in the village of Hsiang T'an, the poster grew in size and amassed a large following after serving as a banner in the war with Japan. Now a charismatic poster, it led troops across China to drive out the armies of Chiang Kai-shek during the civil war, ultimately forcing the Nationalists to Formosa under threat of severe paper cuts.

The new government's Central Governing Council is made up of some of the poster's top advisor-banners, including the new Chinese flag, which features a solid red background with five yellow stars in the corner. The flag is slated to become the nation's second-in-command. The council voted the poster the sole leader of China's new Communist government, granting smaller pictures regional authority over much of the newly unified country. Pocket-sized paper books are slated to be handed to all Chinese citizens to further solidify the poster's control.

A NEW ERA

The giant picture's total control over China marks a distinct departure from traditional Chinese governance. This new era of political power in the hands of poster-imagery was summed up by Yang Shan-kun, a political observer: "This is one of the first times in Chinese history that we have been able to see one of our leaders. In the past, our great emperors were hidden from view in the Forbidden City, but in this new Communist era of humble egalitarianism, the leader has revealed himself to us. And his enormous size and unwavering expression prove to us his greatness."

"How great our poster-leaders of antiquity must have been," Yang continued. "While they were hidden from public view, we can theorize now that they, too, were just as enormous, attractive, fatherly looking, and fixed in their proud, determined gaze."

Sources close to the new government indicate that the poster of Mao may be planning a summit with the marble statue of Josef Stalin by year's end. Some U.S. observers have speculated that a meeting between the Mao poster and newsreel footage of President Truman could happen as soon as the middle of next year.

In such a summit meeting, the poster and the footage would face each other in an ornate room while cameras capture their images to make other pictures.

from Our Dumb Century: 100 Years of Headlines from America's Finest News Source

AMERICA FIRST

First in Oil Consumption:
The United States burns up 20.7 million barrels
<http://www.eia.doe.gov/emeu/cabs/topworldtables3_
4.html> per day, the equivalent of the oil consumption
of China, Japan, Germany, Russia, and India combined.

First in Carbon Dioxide Emissions:
Each year, world polluters pump 24,126,416,000 metric
tons of carbon dioxide (CO_2) into the environment. The
United States
<http://en.wikipedia.org/wiki/List_of_countries_by_ca
rbon_dioxide_emissions> and its territories are
responsible for 5.8 billion metric tons of this, more than
China (3.3 billion), Russia (1.4 billion) and India (1.2
billion) combined.

First in External Debt:
The United States owes $10.040 trillion, nearly a quarter
<https://www.cia.gov/library/publications/the-world-
factbook/rankorder/2079rank.html> of the global debt
total of $44 trillion.

First in Military Expenditures:
The White House has requested $481 billion for the
Department of Defense for 2008, but this huge figure
does not come close to representing total U.S. military
expenditures projected for the coming year. To get a
sense of the resources allocated to the military, the costs
of the global war on terrorism, of the building,
refurbishing, or maintaining of the U.S. nuclear arsenal,
and other expenses also need to be factored in. Military
analyst Winslow Wheeler did the math
<http://www.counterpunch.org/wheeler03072007.html
> recently: "Add $142 billion to cover the anticipated
costs of the wars in Iraq and Afghanistan; add $17 billion

requested for nuclear weapons costs in the Department of Energy; add another $5 billion for miscellaneous defense costs in other agencies.... and you get a grand total of $647 billion for 2008."

Taking another approach to the use of U.S. resources, Columbia University economist Joseph Stiglitz and Harvard Business School lecturer Linda Blimes, added <http://www.rollingstone.com/politics/story/12855294/national_affairs_the_2_trillion_dollar_war> to known costs of the war in Iraq invisible costs like its impact on global oil prices as well as the long-term cost of health care for wounded veterans and came up with a price tag of between 1 trillion and $2.2 trillion.

First in Weapons Sales:
Since 2001, U.S. global military sales have normally totaled between $10 and $13 billion. That's a lot of weapons, but in fiscal year 2006, the Pentagon broke its own recent record, inking arms sales agreements worth $21 billion. It almost goes without saying that this is significantly more than any other nation in the world.

First in Sales of Surface-to-Air Missiles:
Between 2001 and 2005, the United States delivered 2,099 surface-to-air missiles like the "Sparrow" and the "AMRAAM" to nations in the developing world, 20% more than Russia, the next largest supplier.

First in Sales of Military Ships:
During that same period, the U.S. sent 10 "major surface combatants" like aircraft carriers and destroyers to developing nations. Collectively, the four major European weapons producers shipped thirteen. And we were first in the anti-ship missiles that go along with such ships, with nearly double (338) the exports of the next largest supplier Russia (180).

First in Military Training:
A thoughtful empire knows that it is not enough to send weapons; you have to teach people how to use them. The Pentagon plans on training the militaries of 138 nations in 2008 at a cost of nearly $90 million. No other nation comes close.

First in Private Military Personnel:
According to bestselling author Jeremy Scahill <http://www.thenation.com/doc/20070528/scahill>, there are at least 126,000 private military personnel deployed alongside uniformed military personnel in Iraq alone. Of the more than sixty major companies that supply such personnel worldwide, more than 40 are U.S. based.

Compiled in 2007 by Freda Berrigan, Senior Research Associate at the World Policy Institute. First published at www.tomdispatch.com

THE INNER LIFE KNOWS NO CONSTRICTIONS

"All of our technology is the externalization of powers innate in the human organism that tribal shamans and mystics have experienced inwardly by cultivating the inner potentials of consciousness. The inner life knows none of the constrictions of time and space. The journey to other worlds and the adventure of exploring the universe beyond the earthly domain belongs to spiritual awakening, not technological development.

"The return of the cycle back toward the seeding of our culture mirrors the return of that which has been repressed in our psyches. Many of the modern world's symptoms of collapse, its degeneration, corruption, and addictions, can be attributed to the reemergence of the dark, long-repressed tribal aspects of consciousness. The socially destructive use of drugs such as tobacco, alcohol, cocaine, hemp, and opium, which in tribal cultures often played a sacred, initiatic role, shows the dark side of our repressed tribal nature returning. The healthy acceptance of nudity in domestic life and on public beaches, as well as its exploitation in pornography, can both be related to the early stirrings of the return of tribal attitudes. Even after three centuries of widespread rational education, people in every society of the world retain their interest in esoteric and occult phenomena, in a return of consciousness to the psychic aspect of reality. Psychic channeling, witchcraft, and paranormal experimentation can be seen as desperate gropings to restore the communication that tribal societies maintained between the psychic and physical realms.

"Concerned scientists, environmentalists, academics, and government agencies who are committed to 'turning around' our social planning are often applying the same reductionist thought patterns that set civilization on its present course toward self-destruction. The return of the seed is not simply a matter of human choice, it is the inescapable law of cycles, and it cannot be dealt with by devising technological and economic solutions. Plans to reform our industrial economies into renewable-resource, ecologically sensitive societies are like confronting a hurricane with an umbrella. The issues extend far beyond economic and industrial modification."

Robert Lawlor, *Voices of the First Day*

A GREAT POVERTY OF TIME

"In 100,000 to 150,000 years the Aborigines' impact on the fragile environment of Australia has been minimal. The country that colonialists confiscated from them was full of magnificent forests and rich with a variety of flora and fauna.

"Hunting and gathering in Australia was never, as often depicted, a hand-to-mouth desperate survivalism. During the seasons of abundance, even in what would be considered the poorer environments of the western Australian deserts, food quests would occupy only an hour or two each day. Even during drought, a mere two or three hours of collecting by the women would provide a day's food for the entire clan. Their traditional way of life provided more time for the artistic and spiritual development of the entire society. Dance, ritual, music – in short, culture – was the primary activity.

"In our society, the average farmer or office worker has little time for these pursuits. Materialistic industrial societies are caught in a round-the-clock whirl in which people are trapped, day after day, in a breathless grind of facing deadlines, racing the clock between several jobs, and trying to raise children and rush through household chores at the same time. Agriculture and industrialism, in reality, have created a glut of material goods and a great poverty of time. Most people have a way of life devoid of everything except maintaining and servicing their material existence 12 to 14 hours every day.

"In contrast, the Aborigines, who had no need for clothing, agriculture, or architecture, had at their disposal 12 to 14 hours a day for cultural pursuits, while their two to three hours of hunting and gathering provided a more balanced, varied, and nutritious diet than agricultural societies have ever achieved. Aboriginals achieved a higher way of life, both physically and spiritually, by maintaining their daily existence in conformity to the law of their Ancestors."

Robert Lawlor, *Voices of the First Day*

THE GREAT LIE

"We understand that the issue is the land, the issue is the earth. We cannot change the economic system, we cannot change the political system, we cannot change the social system, until the people control the land and then we take it out of the hands of that sick minority that chooses to pervert the meaning and intention of humanity.

"The great lie is that it is civilization. It's not civilized. It has been literally the most bloodthirsty, brutalized system ever imposed upon this planet. That is not civilization. That's the great lie, is that it represents civilization. Or if it does represent civilization and that's truly what civilization is, then the great lie is that civilization is good for us.

"I think we need to put really serious thought into the fact that we're dealing with a disease. You know, it's like there's this predator energy on this planet and this predator energy feeds upon the essence of the spirit, feeds upon the essence of the human being, the spirit. This predator energy takes fossil fuel and other resources out of the earth and turns them into fuel to run a machine system. But in order for there to be a need for that system and in order for that system to work, they have to mine our minds to get at the essence of our spirit.

"The same way the external mining takes place and pollutes – we see now how people understand that it poisons the environment, the water, the air – the mining of the essence, the mining of the spirit, mining our minds, the pollution from that is all the neurotic, distorted, insecure behavior patterns that we develop. That's the pollution. Because in order for this predatory system – this disease – to work, we must not be able to use our minds in a clear, coherent manner. Because if we use our minds in a clear, coherent manner, we will not accept the unacceptable. But it's a disease. It travels through the mind, through the generations."

John Trudell, *Mining Our Minds & the Great Lie (transcribed from audio)*

THE HEART OF MOTHER EARTH

"I, Chief Arvol Looking Horse of the Lakota, Dakota, and Nakota Nations, ask you to understand an Indigenous perspective on what has happened in America, what we call Turtle Island. To understand the depth of this message you must recognize the importance of Sacred Sites and realize the interconnectedness of what is happening today in reflection of the continued massacres that are occurring on other lands and in our own Americas.

"Our people have strived to protect Sacred Sites from the beginning of time. Our ancestors have been trying to protect our Sacred Site called the Sacred Black Hills in South Dakota, "Heart of Everything That Is," from continued violations.

"Our ancestors never saw a satellite view of this site but now that those pictures are available, we see that it is in the shape of a heart and, when fast-forwarded, it looks like a heart pumping. The Dine have been protecting Big Mountain, calling it the liver of the earth, and we are suffering and going to suffer more from the extraction of the coal there and the poisoning processes used in doing so.

"The Aborigines have warned of the contaminating effects of global warming on the Coral Reefs, which they see as Mother Earth's blood purifier. The indigenous people of the rainforest say that the rainforests are the lungs of the planet and need protection.

"The Gwich'in Nation in Alaska has had to face oil drilling in the Arctic National Wildlife Refuge coastal plain, also known to the Gwich'in as "Where life begins." We need to understand the types of minds that are continuing to destroy the spirit of our whole global community. Unless we do this, the powers of destruction will overwhelm us.

"Our Ancestors foretold that water would someday be for sale. Back then this was hard to believe since water was so plentiful, so pure, and so full of energy, nutrition and spirit. Today we have to buy pure water, and even then the nutritional minerals have been taken out; it's just empty liquid. Someday water will be like gold, too expensive to afford. Not everyone will have the right to drink safe water.

"We fail to appreciate and honor our Sacred Sites, ripping out the minerals and gifts that lay underneath them as if Mother Earth were simply a resource instead of the source of life itself. Attacking nations and using more resources to carry out destruction in the name of peace is not the answer! We need to understand how all these decisions affect the global nation; we will not be immune to its repercussions. Allowing continual contamination of our food and land is affecting the way we think. A disease of the mind has set in on world leaders and many members of our global community with their belief that a solution of retaliation and destruction of peoples will bring peace.

"In our prophecies it is told that we are now at the crossroads: either unite spiritually as a global nation or be faced with chaos, disasters, diseases, and tears from our relatives' eyes. We are the only species that is destroying the source of life, meaning Mother Earth, in the name of power, mineral resources, and ownership of land. We use chemicals and methods of warfare that are doing irreversible damage, and Mother Earth is becoming tired and cannot sustain any more impacts of war.

"I ask you to join me on this endeavor. Our vision is for the peoples of all continents, regardless of their beliefs in the Creator, to come together as one at their Sacred Sites to pray and meditate and commune with one another, thus promoting an energy shift to heal our Mother Earth and achieve a universal consciousness toward attaining peace.

"As each day passes, I ask all nations to begin a global effort and remember to give thanks for the sacred food that has been gifted to us by our Mother Earth so the nutritional energy of medicine can be guided to heal our minds and spirits. This new millennium will usher in an age of harmony or it will bring the end of life as we know it. Starvation, war, and toxic waste have been the hallmark of the great myth of progress and development that ruled the last millennium.

"To us, as caretakers of the heart of Mother Earth, falls the responsibility of turning back the powers of destruction. You, yourself, are the one who must decide. You alone – and only you – can make this crucial choice, to walk in honor or to dishonor your relatives. On your decision depends the fate of the entire world.

"Each of us is put here in this time and this place to personally decide the future of humankind. Did you think the Creator would create unnecessary people in a time of such terrible danger? Know that you, yourself, are essential to this world. Understand both the blessing and the burden of that. You, yourself, are desperately needed to save the soul of this world. Did you think you were put here for something else?"

Chief Arvol Looking Horse, *The Heart of the World*

A TRUE REVOLUTION OF VALUES

"A true revolution of values will soon cause us to question the fairness and justice of many of our past and present policies. One day we must come to see that the whole Jericho Road must be transformed so that men and women will not be constantly beaten and robbed as they make their journey on life's highway. True compassion is more than flinging a coin to a beggar. It comes to see that an edifice which produces beggars needs restructuring.

"A true revolution of values will soon look uneasily on the glaring contrast of poverty and wealth. With righteous indignation, it will look across the seas and see individual capitalists of the West investing huge sums of money in Asia, Africa, and South America, only to take the profits out with no concern for the social betterment of the countries, and say, 'This is not just.' The Western arrogance of feeling that it has everything to teach others and nothing to learn from them is not just.

"A true revolution of values will lay hand on the world order and say of war, 'This way of settling differences is not just.' This business of burning human beings with napalm, of filling our nation's homes with orphans and widows, of injecting poisonous drugs of hate into the veins of peoples normally humane, of sending men home from dark and bloody battlefields physically handicapped and psychologically deranged, cannot be reconciled with wisdom, justice, and love. A nation that continues year after year to spend more money on military defense than on programs of social uplift is approaching spiritual death."

Martin Luther King, Jr., *Beyond Vietnam*

DEMOCRATIC CONFEDERALISM

"Democratic confederalism is flexible, multicultural, anti-monopolistic, and consensus-oriented. Ecology and feminism are central pillars. In the frame of this kind of self-administration, an alternative economy will become necessary, one that increases the resources of the society instead of exploiting them and thus does justice to the manifold needs of the society.

"The state continuously orientates itself towards centralism in order to pursue the interests of the power monopolies. Just the opposite is true for confederalism. Not the monopolies but the society is at the center of political focus. Distinct centralism only results in social eruptions.

"The classification of the society in categories and terms after a certain pattern is produced artificially by the capitalist monopolies. What counts in a society like that is not what you are but what you appear to be. Economic, political, ideological, and military monopolies are constructions that contradict the nature of society by merely striving for the accumulation of surplus. They do not create values.

"Essentially, the nation-state is a militarily structured entity. Nation-states are eventually the products of all kinds of internal and external warfare. None of the existing nation-states has come into existence all by itself. Invariably, they have a record of wars. This process is not limited to their founding phase but rather it builds on the militarization of the entire society. The civil leadership of the state is only an accessory of the military apparatus. Liberal democracies even outdo this by painting their militaristic structures in democratic and liberal colors.

However, this does not keep them from seeking authoritarian solutions at the highpoint of a crisis caused by the system itself. Fascist exercise of power is the nature of the nation-state. Fascism is the purest form of the nation-state.

"Democratic confederalism is a non-state social paradigm. It is not controlled by a state. The future will be democratic confederalism."

Abdullah Ocalan, *Democratic Confederalism*

PARIS, MAY '68

"At about 9 pm the first barricades went up spontaneously. Everyone recognized instantly the reality of their desires in that act.

"The hierarchical pyramid had melted like a lump of sugar in the May sun. People conversed and were understood in half a word. There were no more intellectuals or workers, but simply revolutionaries engaged in dialogue. The streets belonged to those who were digging them up.

"Capitalized time stopped. Without any trains, metro, cars or work the strikers recaptured the time so sadly lost in factories, on motorways, in front of the TV. People strolled, dreamed, learned how to live. Desires began to become little by little, reality. For the first time youth really existed."

René Viénet, *Enragés et situationnistes
dans le mouvement des occupations*

THE ANTI-MECHANISTIC NATURE OF ORGANISMS

"Do take note of the radically anti-mechanistic nature of organisms. Mechanical systems work by a hierarchy of controllers and the controlled that returns the systems to set points. One can recognize such mechanistic systems in the predominant institutions of our society. They are undemocratic and non-participatory. Bosses make decisions and workers work, and in between the top and the bottom are 'line-managers' relaying the unidirectional 'chain of command.' Organic systems, by contrast, are truly democratic, they work by intercommunication and total participation. Everyone works and pays attention to everyone else. Everyone is simultaneously boss and worker, choreographer and dancer. Each is ultimately in control to the extent that she is sensitive and responsive. There are no predetermined set points to which the systems have to return. Instead, organisms live and develop from moment to moment, freely and spontaneously. All that is a consequence of the energy stored, aided and abetted by the special physiochemical properties of living matter....

"Remember that stored energy is coherent energy. The organism is, therefore, a highly coherent domain possessing a full range of coherence times and coherence volumes of energy storage. In the ideal, it can be regarded as a quantum superposition of coherent space-time activities, each itself coherent, and coupled to the rest."

Mae-Wan Ho, *The Rainbow and the Worm*

A VISION OF COLLECTIVE HEALING

"I was on an African plain where hundreds of natives were dancing a dance of celebration. (I have no idea why this particular culture was selected.) The lions were far away, there was no danger, there was food and no one was hungry. The tribe had survived the rigors of life for another year and they were dancing their thanks. They were dancing their celebration of life. This was an extraordinary sensation. I was able to take in the experience of these many people whole. I was the tribal mind reveling in celebration. Their infectious joy and dance-induced ecstasy blended them into a single field of celebration. They knew what was happening, and they kept giving themselves over to the process, letting it deepen and deepen until they were completely awash with the unifying joy of their tribe, the plain, the earth, etc. They were one with themselves, each other, and their environment. I had never experienced anything like this before in my life, this melting into a communal embrace, and it was profoundly moving. How impoverished we are that we have lost these rituals that activate the deeper weave of our interconnectedness."

Christopher M. Bache, *Dark Night, Early Dawn*

THE DESTINY OF LOVE

"The idea of actually living community is completely foreign to our culture. Although everyone knows that most marriages and relationships fail, we nevertheless keep trying, again and again. If one relationship doesn't work, maybe the next one will. The attempt to live in a free sexuality outside community often causes more confusion than healing. It is difficult to live in free sexuality outside of a community and it is also difficult to live in lasting, truthful community without truth in sexuality. A group cannot achieve real transparency if the members have to conceal a large part of their inner processes.

"There is a huge longing for the numinous in sexuality and it requires revelation and a fully lived life. The longing for personal love and partnership is still as vast and unsolved today as it was thousands of years ago.

"The power of anonymous Eros and the power of personal love are the forces which need answers that serve healing. They must no longer threaten and fight each other. Neither moral appeals nor old rituals are enough to solve the issues of the longing for love and the longing for anonymous sexuality in our present culture. How will sexuality once more be acknowledged as the sacred force which it actually is in its being and origin?"

Sabine Lichtenfels, *Temple of Love*

WHEN THE RENOWNED PHRYNE SHOWED HERSELF NAKED

"When the renowned Phryne showed herself naked at her trial, her defenders emphasized not so much the aesthetic aspect of her profane beauty but rather her sacred and Aphroditic aspect. The judges were seized with holy fear of the divinity; they dared not condemn the prophetess and priestess of Aphrodite."

Athenaeus, *The Banquet of the Learned*

ERASING PERSONAL HISTORY

"Erasing personal history assumes the termination of the cause/effect relationship between the past and the present.

"This idea seems strange to us not only because we are accustomed to think of the past as forming the foundation of the present, but also because we tend to regard the past as something unchangeable, which gives us a perfect excuse not to change. Most of the time, we justify the past. 'It's that I never learned to discipline myself.' 'It's that I have always been weak.' 'It's that I was over-protected by my parents.' It's that, it's that....And the 'it's that' always has to do with the past.

"Erasing personal history is a magical possibility that is difficult to explain using rational logic. Erase the past— don't try to overcome it, simply erase it. This does not imply that we can erase past events from our lives. Rather it is the breaking of the relationships we have established with them, whose most common modes of expression are in our way of being.

"If personal history is the principal obstacle to change, then the power to erase it represents the doorway to freedom.

"Resistance to behaving in novel ways arises from the belief that we are incapable of doing anything outside the inventory of past actions. And when we try to change, we find personal history to be the major obstacle standing in our way. Family and friends also tend to resist our change; being so familiar with our personal history, they do not allow us to act outside its dictates.

"There is nothing more menacing to the ego than dealing with a person whom we cannot classify. Personal history gives us several labels with which we define our own person. Likewise, we classify everyone around us using labels that we derive from their personal history, real or imaginary. Since we can't deal with the mysterious, we deal with labels.

"We must erase ourselves to the point where we also become a mystery even to ourselves. The loss of certainty as to whom we suppose ourselves to be, which emanates from personal history, is congruent and reciprocal with the loss of certainty as to what we normally consider to be the real world. We find that the reality of the ego and external reality as well are nothing more than descriptions.

"Beyond the description lies the field of the unknown where nothing is written down beforehand; it is not the self or the world. It is the place where we can create, choose, or be anything we want to be. It is the field of freedom."

Victor Sanchez, *The Teachings of Don Carlos*

BEING TAKEN OUT OF BONDAGE

"You have come to alter and remove the frequency of limitation and to bring in the frequency of information. When you are informed, you move beyond the need to be in fear. This new frequency is called knowledge, light, and information. It is called being taken out of bondage. You are being taken out of disinformation and misinformation and you are becoming informed; you are coming into light.

"You believe that you live in the land of the free and the home of the brave, yet you live in the most controlled experimental society on the planet. The tyranny that has been set up here is a tyranny without walls. As a country and a collective consciousness, the United States still has not reached an awareness that something is not right.

"Because everyone is so frightened of giving up the system in the United States, they are going to be *forced* to give it up. The system is corrupt, it does not work, it does not honor life, and it does not honor Earth. That is the bottom line. If something does not honor life and does not honor Earth, you can bet it is going to fall, and it is going to fall big time.

"In the next few years, a connectedness and communal cooperation will begin to run through this country so that you will stop separating yourselves with respect to political ideology. That separation was designed. Whenever a people are separated, and they focus on what they do not have in common or label themselves different from others, it is a perfect disguise to keep them from discovering what they do have in common. This separation keeps people from banding together and becoming strong.

"Reach out and feel the confusion that is spreading around this world about what is going on. This planet has operated on a very low frequency, a frequency based on survival and on disempowerment. Your identity has been based on what you could gather outside of yourself. All of the money saved and property owned – all of the security that provides you with identity – is completely irrelevant to the evolution of the planet.

"Reach your minds out into your communities and feel how the foundation that people have based their lives on is slowly slipping away into rubble. The global grasp of reality is going, going, gone. The foundation is sliding away, and there are those who cannot see the slide at this time. The most significant reason for this slide is that there is new information accessible that makes the old information archaic and decrepit, and you are responsible for this. So you are responsible for being your own forms of inspiration – for being living examples for others.

"There is a need for each of you to examine the boundaries you have set around yourself. You believe that you have evolved, that you have a large picture, and that you see many things. And, relative to where you have journeyed from, indeed you have made progress. However, we guarantee that you are not seeing the boundaries that you presently set for yourself, which still define what you believe you can and cannot do. They are what tethers you to this version or frequency of reality."

Barbara Marciniak, *Bringers of the Dawn*

EVERYONE IS CHOSEN AND EVERYONE KNOWS IT

"Everyone is chosen and everyone knows it, including plants and animals. We seem to be winning and losing but in reality there is no losing. The wiggle of a worm is as important as the assassination of a president."

Agnes Martin, *Agnes Martin Writings*

BEHIND THE WORLD ANOTHER WORLD

"Behind the world another world, stretching away into the wailing shadows, awaited the crumbling of that curious wall which would free all of us."

Kenneth Patchen, *The Journal of Albion Moonlight*

ACKNOWLEDGEMENTS

"The Near Future" and "Now What" first appeared in Arthur Magazine. "If You See Something, Say Something," "Let's Burn the Flags of All Nations," and "After Patriarchy Collapses and Capitalism Crumbles" first appeared on Reality Sandwich, www.realitysandwich.com. "If You See Something, Say Something" also appeared in *Toward 2012: Perspectives on the Next Age* (Tarcher/Penguin, New York, 2008).

"In the Tribe, the Chief is Under Surveillance" by Pierre Clastres, *The Archeology of Violence*. "What Is Patriotism?" by Emma Goldman, *Patriotism: A Menace to Liberty*. "The Original Form of Pollution" by Raoul Vaneigem, *The Movement of the Free Spirit*. "Giant Poster of Mao Seizes Power in China," *Our Dumb Century: 100 Years of Headlines from America's Finest News Source* by Onion Staff, Scott Dikkers. "America First" by Freda Berrigan first appeared on www.tomdispatch.com. "The Inner Life Knows No Constrictions" and "A Great Poverty of Time" by Robert Lawlor, *Voices of the First Day*. "The Great Lie" by John Trudell, *Mining the Minds and the Great Lie*. "The Heart of Mother Earth" by Chief Arvol Looking Horse first appeared in *The Catholic Worker, January 2017*. "A True Revolution of Values" by Martin Luther King, Jr. is taken from "Beyond Vietnam," his speech of April 4, 1967. "Democratic Confederalism" by Abdullah Ocalan, *Democratic Confederalism*. "Paris, May '68" by René Viénet, *Enragés et situationnistes dans le mouvement des occupations*. "The Anti-Mechanistic Nature of Organisms" by Mae-Wan Ho, *The Rainbow and the Worm*. "A Vision of Collective Healing" by Christopher M. Bache, *Dark Night, Early Dawn*. "The Destiny of Love" by Sabine Lichtenfels, *Temple of Love*. "When the Renowned Phryne Showed Herself Naked," Athenaeus, *The Banquet of the Learned*. "Erasing Personal History" by Victor Sanchez, *The Teachings of Don Carlos*. "Being Taken Out of

Bondage" by Barbara Marciniak, *Bringers of the Dawn*. "Everyone Is Chosen and Everyone Knows It" by Agnes Martin, *Agnes Martin Writings*. "Behind the World Another World" by Kenneth Patchen, *The Journal of Albion Moonlight*.

We gratefully acknowledge these sources for fair use of material quoted.

The illustration on the page facing the epigraph is of a Mojica jar, circa 500 a.d., from north coastal Peru.

ABOUT THE AUTHOR

Michael Brownstein grew up rural. His first glimpse of a collective human destiny – urban version – came while taking part in the events of May'68 in Paris. *(People pouring into the streets from out of nowhere without doubt or hesitation...)* Michael is the author of three novels – *Self-Reliance, The Touch,* and *Country Cousins* – as well as ten poetry titles including *World on Fire,* a book-length poem about corporate globalization and consciousness change. ("This outrageous and outraged book challenges the structural violence which has wrapped its fingers around the throat of our suffering world." —Roshi Joan Halifax) He lives in the Catskill mountains.

Philippe Garnier

To the memory of my beloved mentor, the distinguished Brazilian educator, Dr. Emanuel Cicero, born in 1907 in Ubatuba, São Paulo. Rector of the College of Rio Grande do Sul from 1943 to 1978, he died in 1988 in Lisbon.

—Maximiliano Reyes, publisher

-FIM-

DR. CICERO BOOKS